Who Will Care For The Orphan?

WHO WILL CARE

—— *for the* ——

ORPHAN?

*If You Are a United Methodist
It Could Be You!*

WAYNE LAVENDER

NEW YORK

Who Will Care For The Orphan?
If You Are a United Methodist It Could Be You!

© 2016 Wayne Lavender.

Published in New York, New York, by Morgan James Publishing. Morgan James and The Entrepreneurial Publisher are trademarks of Morgan James, LLC.
www.MorganJamesPublishing.com

The Morgan James Speakers Group can bring authors to your live event. For more information or to book an event visit The Morgan James Speakers Group at www.TheMorganJamesSpeakersGroup.com.

Shelfie

A **free** eBook edition is available
with the purchase of this print book.

CLEARLY PRINT YOUR NAME ABOVE IN UPPER CASE

Instructions to claim your free eBook edition:
1. Download the Shelfie app for Android or iOS
2. Write your name in **UPPER CASE** above
3. Use the Shelfie app to submit a photo
4. Download your eBook to any device

ISBN   9781630478551   paperback
ISBN   9781630478575   eBook
ISBN   9781630478568   hardcover
Library of Congress Control Number:
2015917615

Cover Design by:
Chris Treccani
www.3dogdesign.net

Interior Design by:
Chris Treccani
www.3dogdesign.net

In an effort to support local communities and raise awareness and funds, Morgan James Publishing donates a percentage of all book sales for the life of each book to Habitat for Humanity Peninsula and Greater Williamsburg.

Get involved today, visit
www.MorganJamesBuilds.com

DEDICATION

....

According to the World Health Organization, an estimated ten million children die every year from the effects of extreme poverty. This amounts to an average of 26,000 per day.

This book is dedicated to the men and women, clergy and laity, youth to seniors, who see these statistics and strive, through works of mercy, to end this reality. It is dedicated to those who labor for a world of peace and justice.

TABLE OF CONTENTS

ACKNOWLEDGEMENTS

....

For me, the writing of a book is a communal effort. This book would never have come into existence without the support and efforts of untold numbers of persons: I am surrounded by both a "cloud of witnesses" who have gone on before me, and a gaggle of family, friends and colleagues whose critical input, enthusiastic support and faithful service drive me forward.

I am reminded at this time of Mrs. Carol, my 2nd grade Sunday School teacher, who instilled in me a passion for service, and Craig Haight, the pastor of my youth. I grew up through the latter years of the Vietnam War and was blessed to have this man as a pastor who was willing to speak out against that conflict while serving in a conservative, veteran-filled congregation. Rev. Haight reminded each of us of the love of God, the non-violent, mission orientated teaching of Jesus Christ, and the equality of all persons regardless of race, color, ethnicity, gender or name by which they worship God. To Don Jones, a UMC clergy person serving as a college professor of ethics at Drew University, and Robert McAffee Brown, whose tenure as a professor at the Pacific School of Religion coincided with my time there as a student. Other clergy I have walked with through the years include Steve Wall-Smith, C. Dale White, Daniel Berrigan, Clayton Miller, Ken Carder and Greg West.

My mother was and is today a beacon of strength and courage, a woman of deep faith who took me as a child to church *and* civil rights rallies, anti-war protests and soup kitchens where I learned at an early age that faithful religion was more than worship attendance.

I appreciate the support and love of our children. You had faith in me as I changed course mid-career, leaving a secure position in a leap of faith to return to school just as some of you were beginning your college careers. Thank you for sitting in on my presentations, for offering important feedback, for getting me speaking engagements and more.

Finally, a word of thanks to my wife, Linda. Words fail to describe the love, patience and support she has offered through this journey. Traveling the counter-cultural path of peace and service has not always been an easy one, but having you by my side has been more than enough.

FOREWORD

....

The desperate plight of the world's orphans exposes in stark images the misguided priorities of nations and institutions, including the church. Poverty, preventable diseases, violence and war, economic deprivation and exploitation, and geo-political power struggles render millions of the world's children homeless and parentless. With penetrating clarity and prophetic challenge, Wayne Lavender raises a crucial question of this generation: "Who will care for the orphan?"

Orphans represent the most vulnerable among us and their existence calls us to evaluate our own priorities and commitments as individuals, institutions, and nations. Ours is the first generation in human history that has the economic, scientific, and technological means to end poverty and insure that all children have access to the resources necessary to thrive, not only survive. What is lacking is the compelling vision, moral commitment, political will, and viable strategies marshaled in support of the most defenseless among us.

Who Will Care for the Orphan confronts The United Methodist Church and its leaders with a means of breaking out of its institutional narcissism and self-serving renewal strategies. The author recognizes that the plight of the world's poor represents a theological as well as an economic and political crisis. Dr. Lavender knows that renewal comes when the church through the Holy Spirit embodies God's nature and presence and reflects God's priorities as made known in Jesus Christ.

The church is called to embody in its proclamations and practices the nature of God and purposes of God. The God revealed in Scripture and supremely in Jesus Christ has a preferential presence with, concern for, and action on behalf of "orphans, widows, and sojourners (immigrants)." God's call always includes justice on behalf of the most vulnerable, the poor and powerless. To know and serve God is to defend those whom God defends, to be in solidarity with those who suffer, and "to do justice, and to love kindness, and to walk humbly with your God" (Micah 6:8).

In the mid1990s the United Methodist Council of Bishops launched an initiative on "Children and Poverty." Among the stated goals was the following: "To reshape The United Methodist Church in response to the God who is among "the least of these" and the evaluation of everything the church is and does in the light of the impact on children and the impoverished." The foundational goal was the "reshaping" of the denomination in response to the God who lives among those Charles Wesley called "Jesus's bosom friends," those who live in poverty. Many congregation, conferences, agencies and individuals took up the challenge and experienced renewed vitality.

The Episcopal Initiative resulted in many conferences, general agencies, local congregations, and individuals expanding their understanding and response to children in poverty. Several million dollars were raised through an appeal, "Hope for the Children of Africa:" these funds enabled the construction of orphanages and partner schools that provided loving aid to thousands of children displaced by wars and economic devastation. Countless creative ministries emerged in local communities as congregations reached out to welcome "the least of these." Many church leaders become advocates for social policies and programs that incorporated the biblical criteria of justice—enabling the least and most vulnerable to flourish as beloved children of God.

But the Episcopal Initiative on Children and Poverty fell woefully short of its fundamental goal of reshaping the denomination in response to the God who defends orphans, widows, and sojourners! Preoccupation with membership decline in the United States and Europe and concern for institutional "survival" took on a sense of urgency greater than the crisis among children and those who live in poverty. The operational goal became reshaping the denomination in response to institutional decline. Organizational restructuring, numerical growth strategies, and entrepreneurial leadership recruitment and formation schemes moved to the top of the denominational agenda. Rather than evaluating everything the church does in light of the impact on the most vulnerable, increased membership and attendance became the implicit and explicit measure of church vitality and faithfulness.

The focus shifted away from the priority of the *missio Dei* to institutional self-preoccupation. The church became the object of mission rather than the instrument of God's mission. Ministry among children and the poor remained an option among multiple programmatic offerings in a consumerist dominated culture and church; "the orphans, widows, and strangers" continue as objects of alms giving more than recipients and avenues of God's transforming divine presence and grace. Systemic causes of poverty, homelessness, violence, and economic inequality are relegated to specialized agencies or those labeled as "social activists."

Who Will Care for the Orphan is a prophetic call for The United Methodist Church to reorder its priorities in response to the God who defends the weak and most vulnerable. With the analysis of a scholar, the vision of a prophet, the compassion of a pastor, and the passion of a committed disciple of Jesus, Dr. Lavender invites United Methodists to be instruments of justice and shalom! As a trained theologian, pastor, and political scientist, he views care of the orphan through lenses of theology, ecclesiology, economics, and politics. While he provides specific programmatic ideas, Dr. Lavender offers a holistic vision for The United

Methodist Church that has the potential for healing ideological divisions and missional malaise of "the people called Methodists."

—The Reverend Dr. Kenneth L Carder
United Methodist Church Bishop, Retired
Ruth W. and A. Morris Williams Distinguished Professor Emeritus
The Practice of Christian Ministry, Duke Divinity School

INTRODUCTION

....

Religion that is pure and undefiled before God, the Father, is this: to care for orphans and widows in their distress, and to keep oneself unstained by the world.
—JAMES 1:27

Can anything on earth be a greater charity, than to bring up orphans?
—JOHN WESLEY
LETTER TO GEORGE WHITEFIELD, 1770

"In the midst of life we are in death." They are words that have been spoken by thousands of pastors down through the centuries. This phrase is found in "A Service of Committal" from the United Methodist Church's (UMC) Book of Worship, and is one that I used over 400 times during my years as a UMC pastor. Derived from the Latin *media vita in morte summus*, the phrase likely originated in France in the 8th Century and is part of a longer passage:

> Media vita in morte sumus ; quem quaerimus adjutorem, nisi te Domine, qui pro peccatis nostris juste irasceris? Sancte Deus, mnia fortis, mnia et misericors Salvator, amarae morti ne tradas nos.

In the midst of life we are in death: of whom may we seek for succor, but of thee, O Lord, who for our sins art justly displeased? Yet, O Lord God most holy, O Lord most mighty, O holy and most merciful Savior, deliver us not into the bitter pains of eternal death.

"I want to show you this. Candido Justino Zefanis was a young boy of 12 when I met him at the Methodist Orphanage at Teles (Mozambique) in 2002. His story is told here as best as we can discern from what he remembers and what has been gathered from independent sources.

Candido was the ninth and final child of his family. His mother died soon after he was born from birth complications. At age 9, he fell out of a tree where he had been cutting down cocoanuts for his family. He broke his left ankle, but was not taken for medical treatment for 4 – 6 weeks during which time an infection developed. Finally, friends of his family took him to the Methodist Hospital at Chicque,. There a doctor determined the infection was life threatening. He amputated Candido's left leg, just below the knee. Several days later, his father arrived to visit. Upon seeing Candido he walked away saying "This is not my boy. My boy had two legs." Candido was abandoned at the hospital.

He remained at the hospital for approximately 3 months and was fed and cared for by the hospital's staff, but eventually taken to the Teles Orphanage where he was living when I was first introduced to him. Candido was the saddest person I have ever met.

Sadly, these words could be spoken 26,000 times *per day, every day,* over the lifeless bodies of orphans and vulnerable children (OVC) who succumb to the effects of extreme poverty around the planet. These deaths are, almost without exception, avoidable: together, the human family has the resources, technology and capacity to greatly reduce infant and child mortality rates, reproducing in the developing world what has taken place in the rich, developed nations across the planet. Tragically, what we lack, however, is the commitment to make this happen.

Modern medical and technological innovation—in the form of sanitation, vaccinations, potable water and nutrition—have lowered the **infant mortality rate** (deaths of children under the age of 1) in the rich, developed, Organization for Economic Cooperation and Development Nations (OECD) to less than 5 per thousand and the **child mortality rate** (deaths of children under the age of 5) to 7 per thousand. This contrasts sharply with the developing nations, located primarily in the global south, where the **infant mortality rate** runs as high as 150 per 1000 and the **child mortality rate** exceeds 200 per thousand. Acute respiratory infections, diarrhea, measles, malaria and malnutrition linked to extreme poverty continue to take their toll on children through and past the age of 18 in the developing world in great contrast to the OECD nations where these issues are virtually non-existent. This is, in essence, a discussion about location: the odds of a child dying before the age of 18 are approximately fifty times higher if said child is unfortunate enough to have been born in a poor, undeveloped nation.

This staggering reality—*26,000 children die daily around the world from the effects of extreme poverty*—means that eight times more children die every day from the effects of extreme poverty than the total number of persons who were killed in the terrorist attack on September 11, 2001. Consider this:

☐ One child dies **every three seconds** somewhere on planet earth from the effects of extreme poverty.

☐ Twenty children die **every minute** around the world from preventable causes: this is the same number of children who were murdered in Sandy Hook, Connecticut, on December 14, 2012.

☐ 400 children die **every twenty minutes** whose lives could be spared for as little as a dollar per child per day: this is the same number of passengers on a fully loaded Boeing 747.

☐ 1,200 children die **every hour**: this is similar to the number of persons who died on the Titanic (Titanic – approximately 1,500 deaths).

☐ 26,000 children die **every day**: more children die every day around the world than the total number of persons who can attend a concert, hockey, basketball game or circus at Madison Square Garden.

☐ 182,000 children die **every week**: this is approximately the total number of who live in Providence, RI, the capital of that state.

☐ 10 million children die **every year** because of a lack of potable water, vaccines, food and other basic medicine: this is a number equal to the total number of persons the Nazis executed in Germany under Adolf Hitler during the reign of the Third Reich (6 million Jews plus 4 million gypsies, homosexuals, disabled persons and others the Nazis considered inferior).

The ongoing death toll of these children rarely makes news in the mainstream media, in faith-based publications, in the blogosphere, worship services or in personal conversations. Out of sight and out of mind for most of us in the developed world, we turn a blind eye to the suffering of these little ones whose very care we—as global citizens, persons of faith, Christians and members of the United Methodist Church—are responsible for. These are real deaths of real children taking place during our lifetimes despite our propensity for collective denial and a shared refusal to accept moral responsibilities. These deaths occur all around the globe but are primarily centered in the undeveloped nations of the global south. The angel of death hovers over these children in the favelas of South America, in the slums of India, in the villages and cities of Africa and beyond.

Parallel and overlapping the tragic death of these 26,000 children per day is the crisis of orphans, of children being raised without one or both parents. Although reliable data is difficult to find a recent UN Report estimates that there are up to 210,000,000 orphans worldwide, and that every day 5,760 more children become orphans. War, AIDS, malaria, cholera, famine, environmental degradation and the misman-agement and or corruption of governing institutions have created condi-tions of extreme poverty and communities filled with orphaned children and teenagers.

The suffering of children around the planet—from the death of 10 million children per year to the existence of 210 million orphans alive and struggling to survive—should elicit an unparalleled response from people of faith all around the world instead of the collective sigh and shrug of our shoulders it usually generates. Seriously, how can any fol-lower of Jesus Christ not be affected and moved to action by these facts?

There is no simple answer to this question. On a daily basis we hear of wars, death and destruction: there are always stories in the news of sex-ual abuse, disease, natural disasters, car/train/airplane accidents, school shootings, police brutality. No matter which way we turn, there are more victims to help, worthy causes to support, rallies to attend, and rights to protect. And we have helped: we have walked and sponsored friends in CROP Walks, we have worked at soup kitchens and overnight shelters, we have sponsored children through agencies where, "for $3 per day you can save a child;" we have paid our World Service apportionments and given to special UMCOR Disaster Responses through specific Advance requests. We have participated and supported others in Volunteers In Mission (VIM) Teams, have sponsored missionaries and given to pro-grams such as the "Imagine No Malaria Campaign." We have engaged in all forms of fundraising, from pancake breakfast to spaghetti suppers, from car washes to the sale of chocolate and wrapping paper. We have held walk-a-thons, sit-a-thons, dance-a-thons and fast-a-thons. We have given and we have helped—to be sure.

But the problems still persist. In fact, they are probably getting worse. It is obvious that the world's needs are greater than our personal or denominational resources. And, because we cannot address all of these issues, we sometimes retreat and neglect to address *any* of them. Instead of using our time, talents, gifts and resources to help where we are capable of making a difference we, as individuals, avoid the mission field altogether and choose, instead, to mulch our garden, renovate the kitchen or build a new storage shed in an effort to feel that we are at least accomplishing something. As a denomination our collective apathy towards helping the human condition around the planet is sidetracked by interdenominational quarreling or the ongoing quest for church growth.

But while these activities might salve our conscience for a while we know, on a deeper level, that the call to true discipleship demands far more. We will not solve the world's problems through fundraisers. The world has some significant problems. United Methodists could take a lead role in addressing these concerns, but we have been too busy with other issues and, to an extent, discouraged and disillusioned. If we change our minds and our approach and return to a Wesleyan theology and methodology, however, we can help lots of people, including ourselves. We can contribute greatly towards building a world of peace with justice and, through our faithful service and sacrifice, attract millions of new members. Wouldn't this be a great direction for a world with children in great need and our struggling denomination?

The United Nations Children's Fund (UNICEF) defines an "orphan" as a person under the age of 18 who has lost at least one parent. Most Americans think that an orphan is a child under 18 who has lost both parents: internationally, a child who has lost one parent is considered an orphan and a child whose mother and father have both died is considered a "double orphan." A maternal orphan is a child whose mother has died and a paternal orphan one whose father had died. While it is obvious that a double orphan, in most circumstances, will suffer more than a maternal or paternal orphan, conditions in the developing world often make it extremely difficult for a child who has lost even one parent to become successful or, in too many circumstances, even survive. In nations where the competition for resources is fierce and the life expectancy hovers around the age 50, as it does in most of Sub-Saharan Africa, the loss of one parent usually creates a crisis—the loss of both parents is often catastrophic.

The word "orphan" is mentioned 41 separate times in the Bible, usually with the admonition to "care for the widow and orphan." There was often a direct relationship between widows and orphans in Biblical times: when a husband / father died leaving behind a wife and child (ren) these surviving family members were often hard-pressed to stay alive. The father was usually the breadwinner who received compensation for his work: a widow and children would be in dire straits if there were no other males in the family to take them in.

While there have been many technological innovations and social changes in the centuries since the Bible was written, many things have remained the same. In a great majority of nations around the world the man is still expected to work and be the primary source of income for the family. Even in the developed nations of Europe and North America there is a lingering assumption that the male is responsible for working outside of the home while the woman may or may not have a career / job. Families that lose their husband/father, whether in Biblical times or today, are at a tremendous disadvantage over those where the husband/father survives.

Think for a moment of your father (if you are fortunate enough to remember him) and think of how you and or your family might have been had he died while you were young. In most cases your father's absence would have created a gaping hole.

Young women / mothers also die: historically, many women died during childbirth, thus leaving their newborn babies maternal orphans. While the number of women dying in childbirth in the developed, wealthy nations has decreased dramatically since the advent of modern medicine, many women in the global south still perish giving birth. There is a long list of other reasons women die young in the poor nations, ranging from disease (malaria and HIV / Aids are still lethal killers in the global south) to accidents, cancers, heart disease, stroke, etc.

Mothers have traditionally filled the role of family nurturer. They have provided the intimate, caring atmosphere in which children experience love and acceptance. Children raised without a mother are often poorly equipped emotionally and may lack the confidence or self-esteem that children raised in a home with their mothers develop.

Think for a moment of your mother (if you are fortunate enough to remember her) and think of how you and or your family might have been had she died while you were young. In most cases your mother's absence would have created a tremendous void.

Orphans, be they maternal, paternal or double, are often children at risk. While the old adage tells us that children are "tough," the loss of a parent at a young age is always traumatic and will leave lasting damage. Many orphans in the rich, developed nations carry emotional baggage with them their entire lives, beginning with depression, reactive attachment disorder, PTSD, anxiety, low self-esteem and difficulty building relationships with superiors, colleagues, friends or spouses. These wounds can, in many circumstances, be healed through counseling, therapy, unconditional love from other family members and the gift of time, but the scar is always present.

For orphans in the global south, however, the emotional trauma of parental loss is often outpaced by the child's physical struggle to survive. Children whose mothers or fathers die in the poor nations of the world usually have two strikes against them, 1) being born in a poor nation and 2) the loss of one or both parents. The primary negative outcomes of becoming an orphan in the global south include, but are not limited to, severe-malnutrition, above-average rates of morbidity and mortality, lower-than-average rates of school attendance and completion at the primary level, and, in all probability, a heavier work burden (both paid and unpaid child labor) (Subbarao and Coury 2004:2).

The circumstances and conditions that orphans have experienced since the dawn of human history have always made it difficult for these children to survive and be successful, but current conditions around the world have magnified these obstacles. Due to a number of historic, cultural, geo-political and economic factors over thirty percent of the world's population—some 2.6 billion persons—live below, at or just above the line of extreme poverty. Extreme poverty, originally defined by the United Nations in 1995, is "a condition characterized by severe deprivation of basic human needs, including food, safe drinking water, sanitation facilities, health, shelter, education and information. It depends not only on income but also on access to services." (United Nations 1995)

Conditions vary, nation-to-nation, region-to-region, continent-to-continent, urban to suburban and rural, but the World Bank has established US$1.25 per day as the threshold for extreme poverty. Approximately 1.4 billion persons live on less than US$1.25 per day, and another billion humans live between US$1.25 and US$2.00 per day.

Those living below this threshold, approximately one sixth of the world's population, lack the resources to fulfill basic human needs: they "survive" on one bowl of rice per day, live in substandard housing and have virtually no health care. (Trickle Up Staff 2014) Those living just over this level fare little better: while $2 per day goes further in the developing world than in the US or Western Europe, raising a family of 4 on US$8 per day is problematic no matter where you live.

These 2.6 billion persons around the planet who live on less than US$2 per day subsist without any financial safety net. They can survive, albeit barely, when food, gas, oil or other commodities increase modestly in price but their very existence is threatened when larger shocks such as dramatic price spikes, droughts, floods, hurricanes, tsunamis, factory closings or serious illness disturb the status quo. When you live on the margins without any savings, insurance, pension, emergency plan or backup strategy unforeseen challenges often have deathly consequences.

Among these 2.6 billion persons living below, at, or just above the line of extreme poverty, 40 percent, approximately 1 billion, are children. Said another way: one billion children around the world live in conditions of extreme poverty.

Children, like their parents or other adults, who live in these conditions live one illness away from death. Children living in extreme poverty don't enjoy the medical, dental, educational, housing or dietary benefits children living in relative comfort take for granted. Children living in extreme poverty are generally unable to receive a basic education. Children who live in extreme poverty live on the margins of survival.

When a child living in extreme poverty loses a parent, or both parents, his or her chances of survival are greatly mitigated. These children, now orphans, constitute the base and largest contributor towards the 26,000 children who die daily around the planet. And, tragically, the number of orphans around the world is increasing. (Subbarao and Coury 2004:xiii)

The Four Horsemen of the Apocalypse, usually portrayed as Conquest, War, Famine and Death, ride at liberty across the planet, virtually unchecked by representatives of institutional religions who are often more focused on theological infighting than self-sacrificial works of mercy. Will we—as the human family—continue to ignore this ongoing tragedy, or will we find another way?

|||||||||||||||||||||||||||||||||||||||||||||||||||||||||||||||||||||||||||||||||||||

Meanwhile, . . . the United Methodist Church is in great crisis (at least within the US and Europe). Bishop Wilke came to this same conclusion in his 1986 book *And Are We Yet Alive*. Lyle Shaller addressed the issue again in his 2004 book, *The Ice Cube is Melting*, and it is painfully obvious to anyone concerned with our denomination. The decline in attendance, membership, youth, income and influence continues apace. John Wesley once worried about the denomination's future when he wrote: "I am not afraid that the people called Methodists should ever cease to exist either in Europe or America. But I am afraid lest they should only exist as a dead sect, having the form of religion without the power. And this undoubtedly will be the case unless they hold fast both the doctrine, spirit, and discipline with which they first set out." Today we should be concerned as to whether the denomination will survive in any form.

The reality is this: our obsessive focus on church growth for the past two decades has been ineffective. It does not matter how many coffee mugs we deliver, how many attractive visitor brochures we give away or how many creative television and advertising campaigns we run, the denomination will not rekindle the Wesleyan flame without a tangible connection to the Biblical message of disciple making, Christian Education, spirituality and a counter-cultural message of self-sacrificial mission work that is all but lost in our consumer-based society.

The United Methodist Church is not united. Partisan fighting, special interest groups and contentious caucuses have created divisive chasms between the progressive and conservative wings of the denomination where the center can no longer be heard. A church divided cannot stand, let alone speak to or solve the persistent challenges facing the human family at this critical time. It is said that Nero fiddled while Rome burned: United Methodists conduct debates while the world waits.

The denomination has reached, I believe, a critical point in our journey where continuing to travel down this same road will lead to further malaise and decline, a shrinking base and reduced local, state, national and international impact. Albert Einstein defined insanity as "doing the same thing over and over again and expecting different results." We must change direction now if we ever want to be a relevant denomination again.

We can do this by finding a common message / mission / ministry. This is simply the best way in which we can incarnate our denominational name as the *United* Methodist Church. We can be the denomination that focuses on orphans and vulnerable children (OVC)—and by leveraging our combined strength we can greatly mitigate the suffering of these innocents.

At the same time, we must sometimes agree to disagree on theological, political and social issues. We must understand the difference between having different opinions on various topics and having outright divisions in the body of Christ that keep us from fulfilling our mission and ministry. As individuals within this denomination we cannot all agree on every theological, political or social issue—but we can unite in service to minister to OVC—something on which progressive and conservatives, Democrats, Republicans and Independents, clergy and laity, young and old can all agree.

Billy Graham once called the United Methodist Church "our country's greatest hope for evangelization in the future," and Robert Schuller described our denomination as a "sleeping giant." (Wilke 1986:86) But first we must stem our sectarian quarreling, unite around a central message and be about the ministry of reforming "the nation and, in particular, the Church; to spread scriptural holiness over the land."

Serendipitously, we can turn our denomination around through a return to John Wesley's theology and methodology. He provided us with the theological framework, economic perspective, personal practices and ecumenical spirit to be as successful in the 21st Century as we were in the 18th and 19th Centuries. The key to our success can be found—again—within! We have Wesley's journal, sermons, personal practices and worldview. John Wesley, founder of the Methodist Movement, had an eternally contemporary message and interpretation of the Bible and understanding of Christianity that is as relevant today as it was 250 years ago.

I submit this proposition to both clergy and laity within the UMC "*connexion*:" we can change our denominational trajectory, and we can change the world! We can both save a significant number of children who are dying by turning our full missional power to this crisis and, BTW, save our denomination at the same time. We can become THE denomination that cares and serves orphans and vulnerable children. We can become THE church that is *united* around a central mission. We can become THE saints of our time, addressing a critical moral and ethical issue of the 21ˢᵗ century.

This book is written for my clergy brothers and sisters who hear that "still small voice" and yearn for more than an endless stream of meetings, potluck dinners, empty pews and fundraisers. Too many clergy, for far too long, experience burn out and compassion fatigue: our personal fires flicker and sputter and are at risk of being extinguished by the slightest breeze. The enthusiasm, courage, energy and vision that many clergy I know began their careers with have faded: many clergy, underpaid, overworked, underappreciated and overwhelmed, are literally finished. Service to OVC can relight these personal flames and spread them throughout the denomination.

This book is written for concerned laity as well, from people like my mother, a five-generation, died-in-the-wool, octogenarian Methodist whose life has always centered around the church to the most recently confirmed young person who is just beginning his or her journey in faith. It is for the men and women who have tithed on every dollar they have ever earned for as long as they can remember, and for the tippers who are waiting for a significant cause worthy of their hard earned income. It is for people who know that there is something bigger out there than the support of a dying institution where salaries, heating and electric bills and apportionments need to be paid. It is for those who have been on Volunteer in Mission (VIM) trips to the developing world and have seen extreme poverty with their own eyes: it is for others who have served at food pantries, overnight shelters and soup kitchens and looked into the eyes of those who live in deep poverty within the USA, the richest nation in the history of the world. It is for those who have seen the growing crisis of children walking towards the US border and understand that this is not a political problem but a humanitarian and spiritual problem, and a problem all of the world's citizens should be concerned with. It is for those who see Jesus in the least, the last and the lost and for those who understand that service to the least, the last and the lost can lead us back to God.

The prescription I offer in these pages for denominational resurrection will work because they worked for Wesley and they worked for me. For twelve years I served as the pastor of a typical United Methodist Church in suburban Connecticut. We had church members of all stripes and types, from every perspective on the political and religious spectrum. We had conservative Republicans and progressive Democrats and frustrated Independents: we had Biblical literalists, persons who read the Bible symbolically, and seekers who were encountering the Bible for the first time and not sure what to believe. We discussed and debated every issue. But the one thing we agreed on was service to those in need.

These experiences, I am convinced, drove our church growth. From a starting point of 80 per week when I arrived in 1993 we grew steadily in faith and service, surpassing the 300 mark around the year 2000. I worked hard to foster the means of grace though works of piety and works of mercy. We created a Mission Community where outreach to the least, the last and lost was encouraged: church members created our own food pantry, volunteered in the local community to serve at the overnight shelter and soup kitchen, ministered to the street people of New York City, sent youth to Appalachia and adults to hurricane-devastated locations in the US. We volunteered at Habitat for Humanity construction sites and in school classrooms, and volunteered at blood banks and visited shut-in seniors. During this time we were able to extend our physical plant with a $1 million addition.

But it was our Mozambique experience in meeting Jesus in the mission field that had the most profound and transformational affect on our church. From my initial trip in 1998 followed a dozen other church members who traveled to this Sub-Saharan nation poor in resources but rich in spirit. From these trips came the decision to raise $85,000 to construct a new home for 25-orphaned children living in the worst conditions imaginable. This mission—raising funds to build an orphanage in Mozambique—generated a level of excitement and energy I have rarely experienced that spread throughout the community and fed our church growth. It is a recipe I believe can be replicated across the denomination.

I discovered a simple truth: theological and political disputes pale in the presence of human suffering—and the willingness and ability to serve those in need creates ties that bind Christians from the right and left together in ways that put theological conflicts in context of what is truly important. We did not all agree on who should be elected to public office, on the evidence for global climate change, need for universal health care or need for same sex marriage equality, but we agreed to care for these children. We can create the beloved community if we are willing to re-order our priorities by focusing on the lives of orphans and vulnerable children— a Biblical and Wesleyan path where great opportunities await.

Christianity is not a spectator religion. It is not a religion for passive pew potatoes, but designed for activists. Mission work, aka John Wesley's works of mercy—when grounded in works of piety as the means of grace—is the balm to save lives and our denomination.

This book, then, is offered as an alternative to the interdenominational quarrelling that has plagued our denomination for the past 30 + years. It is a book by a United Methodist pastor for the United Methodist Church about how we can relight the Wesleyan fire across the denomination. It is not a book about orphans, per se, but a book about how service to orphans and vulnerable children—through works of mercy—can provide us, individually and collectively, the means of grace necessary for growth and development.

CHAPTER I

Whither the UMC

Jesus said: "Let the little children come to me, and do not stop them; for it is to such as these that the kingdom of heaven belongs."
—MATTHEW 19: 14

Permit me, sir, to give you one piece of advice. Be not so positive; especially with regard to things which are neither easy nor necessary to be determined. When I was young I was sure of everything. In a few years, having been mistaken a thousand times, I was not half so sure of most things as I was before. At present, I am hardly sure of anything but what God has revealed to man.
—JOHN WESLEY
A LETTER TO THE EDITOR OF THE "LONDON MAGAZINE," 1765

I had the opportunity to attend the final worship service of a United Methodist Church last year. The urban church, which averaged 600 in worship and over 1,000 in Sunday School through the 1950's and 1960's, had declined to where its average worship attendance hovered around 10: its Sunday School disbanded years ago. The bishop, superintendent, pastor and former pastors participating in this solemn service, surpassed the folks in the pews who attended this finale. The mood was somber and the spoken words, taken from the UMC Book of Worship's "Order For the Leave-Taking of a Church Building" and "An Order for Disbanding a Congregation" echoed around the empty corners of what once was a beautiful and vibrant sanctuary. The facility itself—in dire need of maintenance deferred through years of decline—will be torn down and replaced with multi-family housing units: the stain glass windows, pipe organ, pews and other items of value will be auctioned off with resulting funds going to a conference mission account.

"I want to show you this: Avan was a 12-year old double orphan living at the UN Sponsored Domiz Refugee Camp near Dohok, Iraq when I met her in 2013. I was leading a group of 12 Kurdish-Iraqi students on a mercy trip to the camp; we brought food, clothing, and school supplies that the students had gathered during the previous weeks, plus 500 envelopes containing the equivalent of 10 US Dollars in Iraqi dinars to give each student for treats at the local store (we also had 20 envelopes filled with 15 US Dollars in Iraqi dinars for their teachers). Avan's parents had both been killed by the Syrian government under the regime of Bashar al-Assad for participating in the pro-democracy protests during the so-called Arab Spring that swept the Arab nations beginning in 2010, arriving in Syria in late 2011. Family members, who were themselves fleeing the vicious civil war that erupted, took her to the camp, and they all (nine total) lived in a 12'x12' tent. They had lived in the camp for 8 months when I met them. Parentless, living in a tent with 8 others in a refugee camp designed for 10,000 persons where in reality over 40,000 persons currently reside, it is difficult to predict Avan's future."

The loss of this church, once the "tallest steeple" and best pastoral appointment in its conference, is being repeated across the United States on a weekly basis. While there are, to be sure, still vital and vibrant UM churches across the *connexion*, the overall trend of the denomination has been one of steep decline. Small churches that never attracted more than 30 worshippers, large churches that in the day sat a thousand in their pews, urban, suburban and rural churches, churches in red and blue states, churches on the east coast, Midwest, mountain and west coast, churches in the north and in the south—in every and all demographic slices of the United States UMCs and failing and falling. We are a denomination in a death spiral.

"The United Methodist Church is a church in crisis," Bishop Richard Wilke wrote in 1986. Wilke documented the decline of the denomination from 1962 through 1984 in his well-read book, *And Are We Yet Alive?* (Wilke 1986) His research, based on annual conference data (one thing our denomination does well is to collect data: we have done this since the time of John Wesley), showed not only an overall declining trend but also indicated that we were an aging denomination among both clergy and laity with decreasing numbers in Sunday School, baptisms, confession of faiths, confirmation classes and more. Wilke warned that unless drastic measures were taken, the decline would continue and even accelerate in the succeeding decades because as our older members retire and die they were not being replaced with members of younger generations.

Two decades later, the declining trend unabated, Lyle Shaller confronted the same issue in his aptly titled book, "The Ice Cube is Melting." (Shaller 2004) Shaller, using the metaphor of a melting ice cube to portray our shrinking denomination, posted a list of divisive topics and questions that he described had led to "Interdenominational Quarreling," i.e. a divided church and, as a result, declining membership:

☐ Human sexuality.

☐ Do long-term financial subsidies nurture creativity or encourage dependency?

☐ Conflict between Anglos and ethnic minorities over priorities.

☐ The role of women in the church.

☐ The responsibility of district superintendents.

☐ Should mega churches be encouraged or discouraged?

☐ What are the values that drive American foreign policy?

☐ Should the UMC declare itself to be one of the peace churches in American Christianity?

☐ Should racial integration of congregations be a high priority?

☐ Should youth ministries focus on teenagers or on family constellations?

☐ How should our church lead in the alleviation of poverty?

☐ What is the role of lay ministry?

☐ How should the denomination confront racism? (Shaller 2004:89)

The decline in membership is disheartening for those concerned with and committed to the UMC. In 1968, when the United Methodist Church came into existence (a result of the merger between the Methodist Church and United Evangelical Church), our denomination had approximately 11 million members. (Alexander 2012:20) At the same time, the US population was roughly 200,000,000. By 2014 membership within the denomination had dropped to 7,299,753 members. In 2014, the US population had grown to 320,000,000.

Some simple math shows that from 1968 – 2014, a period of 46 years, our denomination lost over 3.5 million members while the United States population grew by 120 million persons. The percent of the US population who were members of the UMC in 1968 was 5.5 percent (11 million members ÷ 200 million population = 5.5%) while in 2014 that percentage had dropped to 2.3 percent (7.3 million ÷ 320 million = 2.3%).

The trend is even more telling when extended over a greater time period. "Between 1776 and 1806 Methodist ranks in the United States increased by 2,500 percent—from 4,900 adherents to 130,000 . . . By 1850 populist outreach had made Methodists the largest denomination, with 2.7 million members." (Phillips 2006:109) Fink and Stark describe our phenomenal growth with these words:

> But the major shift in the American religious market in this period was the meteoric rise of Methodism. In 1776 the Methodists were a tiny religious society with only 65 churches [I think the authors mean meeting or preaching houses] scattered through the colonies. Seven decades later they towered over the nation. In 1850 there were 13,302 Methodist congregations, enrolling more than 2.6 million members—the largest single denomination, accounting for more than a third of all American church members. (Finke and Stark 1992:56)

If the current trends continue our slide towards irrelevancy will be complete by the year 2050: in that year the US population is expected to exceed 400 million persons while the UMC membership will drop below 4 million members, meaning that less than 1 percent of Americans will be members of our denomination. Unless something dramatic takes place, there will be many more opportunities in the years ahead in which we can participate in an "Order For the Leave-Taking of a Church Building" and "An Order for Disbanding a Congregation" from our Book of Worship.

A CHURCH DIVIDED

I was ordained a deacon and probationary member of the New York Annual Conference of the United Methodist Church on June 9, 1984, in the auditorium of the University of Bridgeport, in Bridgeport, Connecticut. Though that event took place over 30 years ago, I can recall vividly many memories of that day, including the robe I wore (given to me by a clergy widow from a church I served as a student pastor), the stole placed over my shoulders by childhood pastor and mentor (purchased and given by my mother—this stole was handmade in Guatemala and purchased at a mission table at annual conference), the embarrassing mistake our bishop made because he had missed rehearsal the night before, the sermon delivered by a guest bishop from a neighboring conference, my class of deacons and the attendance of family and friends who were there to support me and others on this important occasion.

But I remember the contentious debate that took place in the time directly preceding our ordination service even better.

It was, as I recall, one of the first times the New York Annual Conference had dealt publically, on the floor of the conference, with the topic of homosexuality. It was a sign of decades of debate to follow.

To his credit, our presiding bishop allowed this debate to run a full 60 minutes. To his detriment, however, the bishop allowed the tone of the debate to become nasty and personal. The debate was memorable for its angry, hate-filled statements, personal attacks and Biblical quoting by persons on both sides of this theological divide. Superintendents, pastors and laity all took part in this contentious discussion, while the gentle persons of grace and love who often offered calming words of reconciliation remained on the sidelines. The debate took place among the delegates to that annual conference, but also in front of many guests and visitors who had arrived early for the ordination service and were invited to sit in the visitor's section outside the voting bar.

Finally, the debate came to an end. The bishop announced a 60 minute break in which the stage was set for the ordination service. We gathered an hour later for that worship service in the auditorium still emotionally charged from the debate. Superintendents, clergy and laity who had spoken during the debate were on the stage singing hymns, leading the liturgy, reading the scriptures, recognizing those who were retiring and, finally, participating in the ordination rite itself. My ordination was clouded by the toxic words spoken in the hour prior to the ordination: rather than a celebratory service of ordination and commissioning, it was a tension filled ceremony with everyone concerned how this fracture would play out in the coming weeks and months. Little did I know that we would still be debating this issue 30 years down the road.

I use this story as a metaphor for the United Methodist Church. Since at least 1984 our denomination has spent more time, energy and funds discussing this issue than it has engaging any other theological topic. It is, in many respects, the perfect theological storm: this is the theological lightning rod from which persons on both sides of the theological and political spectrum choose to stand. Seen from both perspectives, this ongoing debate has created a great amount of pain and frustration. It is also a topic that has distracted us and diverted many resources to this cause from life-saving activities, such as service to orphans and vulnerable children. It is a topic that the mainstream media picks up on and shares with the society at large: this debate, I submit, contributes to our overall decline as outside observers see the UMC as a deeply divided and divisive denomination.

Those who support marriage equality and full rights for the LGBTQ community see this as a civil rights issue akin to our discussions and debate 150 years earlier on the topic of slavery, revisited some 50 years ago during the Civil Rights Movement for racial equality. They point to the millions of young persons who are turned off by a denomination that does not have an open and affirming policy regarding human sexuality. They argue that in a nation where marriage equality is the law of the land how can we, as a denomination, refuse to perform same sex marriages? And while acknowledging that there are a handful of scriptural texts that prohibit homosexuality, they claim these passages are either misunderstood or set in a cultural context that does not reflect God's will—pointing to other scriptural passages such as the dietary laws of the

Old Testament or the seemingly acceptable practice of slavery within the scriptures—as examples where we do not follow Biblical standards.

Those opposed to marriage equality and full rights for LGBTQ people see this as a threat to their theological worldview and appeal to scripture, reason, experience and tradition for ultimate justification. God created Adam and Eve, man and women, for marriage, reproduction and companionship, they say. Anything else is a violation of God's will and an affront to God that will bring down His righteous judgment on our society and institutions. The Bible is clear: homosexuality is an abomination and must therefore incompatible with Christian teaching.

This is an important theological topic. Theology matters. All religions / denominations have theological foundations—these foundations help explain who we are, what we believe, and how we are different from other religions and denominations. The United Methodist Church is a monotheistic, Christian, Protestant religion founded on the Biblical record as revealed in the Hebrew Scriptures (Old Testament) and New Testament. We declare ourselves to be disciples of Jesus Christ and followers of John Wesley, our spiritual founder. We are not Jews, who do not accept that Jesus of Nazareth was the Messiah. Likewise, we are not Muslims, who believe that Jesus was a prophet in a long line of prophets culminating in Mohammed, through whom the Qur'an was "revealed" that is now the central text of that religion. While we agree with other Christians on many subjects, we also disagree with them: for instance, our Roman Catholic brothers and sisters accept seven sacraments to our two, are led by a single person—the Pope—who is considered the keeper of the faith and in direct line with St. Peter, ordain only men while we ordain men and women, and have their clergy take vows of chastity, poverty and obedience while our ordination promises are less dramatic, if just as binding.

Theology matters in that it helps create and forge identity and worldview. Theology helps shape who we are and what we believe in. It is important.

But theology is also divisive and often generates great disagreement. There are some very important theological questions in which members of the United Methodist Church, like members of other Christian organizations, do not all agree on, including:

☐ Do you have to be a Christian, i.e. a believer in Jesus Christ, to enter heaven?

☐ Are all of the stories of the Bible literally true: did they really take place?

☐ Does hell exist?

☐ Does Satan exist?

☐ Should Christians practice birth control?

☐ What is baptism, who is it for, and should infants be baptized?

☐ Should Christians drink alcohol? Take recreational drugs?

☐ How do we understand Jesus' teachings on non-violence?

It was, in part, theological differences between Christians and Muslims that led to the Crusades of the Middle Ages, and theological differences between Protestants and Catholics that led, in part, to the ferocious violence of the French Wars of Religion and Thirty Years War. It is Pascal who is attributed to this damning phrase, "Men never do evil so completely and cheerfully as when they do it from religious conviction," and Noble Prize winning author Steven Weinberg who once wrote: "With or without religion, good people can behave well and bad people can do evil; but for good people to do evil — that takes religion."(Weinberg 1999)

There will be no war between members of the UMC who hold different positions on theological issues. In the years since my ordination I have seen countless debates on this topic, from small group discussions at local churches to the showdown every four years at General Conference. I have witnessed great anger and frustration, but have also seen, from time to time, a genuine concern and friendship between persons of differing viewpoints. There are, certainly, persons of great integrity and intellect on both sides of this divide. So, while we won't go to actual war over this topic, we will continue to debate and divide over it.

A person in favor of marriage equality and the ordination of gays and lesbians is likely to be a person with a progressive, liberal understanding of the Bible. A person against marriage equality and the ordination of gays and lesbians is more likely to be a person with a traditional, conservative, literal understanding of the Bible. Their worldviews collide on this and other theological topics. A truce could be established, however, between these two camps where they put their theological differences aside and agree to serve orphans and vulnerable children.

"Candido's Story, continued:

The orphanage at Teles where I first met Candido was literally at the end of the earth. It had no running water, no electricity and no access to health care or schools. The children were sickly and constantly hungry with virtually no contact with the outside world. The orphanage had previously been a leper's colony, abandoned in the 1960's because medicine had eliminated the necessity for such facilities. The site was up a short hill from a swamp where malaria-infested mosquitos bred. It was a location that offered little hope to the unfortunate children who had entered and resided there–and Candido was no exception.

And yet, I saw something in this boy that let me know he was special. Pictured here at Teles in 2002, wearing a silly hat and sunglasses and playing with a soccer ball we brought from the US, Candido was able to get around by alternatively hopping and using those miserable and undersized crutches as well as most children move with two legs. He once "ran away" from the orphanage and they eventually found him eight miles away on the road leading back to the hospital. He had spirit; he just needed to catch a break.

On the flight back to the US, I thought a lot about Candido and about the possibility of adopting him. I was the father of three boys about his same age. If anyone could bring him to the US and adopt him, I thought it could be me. I felt as though God was calling me to adopt Candido."

THE CHILDREN OF ATHENS AND THE CHILDREN OF JERUSALEM

James Nuechterlein gives credit to Otto Paul Kretzmann for creating a metaphor for understanding the theological chasm separating members of the UMC and Christians in general: it is the metaphor of the Children of Athens and the Children of Jerusalem. (Nuechterlein 1988) Lyle Schaller uses this metaphor in his book, *The Ice Cube is Melting*. The metaphor is brilliant and well chosen. Athens and Jerusalem are ancient cities associated with different perspectives and worldviews.

Children of Athens tend to be those who focus on human knowledge and learning, associated with Athens because of its philosophical history and tradition. Athens was the birthplace of Western Philosophy and home of, among others, to Socrates, Plato and Aristotle.

In this metaphor the Children of Athens are represented in Wesley's Quadrilateral under the banner of "Reason." Raphael's *The School of Athens,* located in the Apostolic Palace of the Vatican, is one of his most famous frescoes and represents the contribution of Philosophy to humanity: it is the perfect embodiment of human learning.

Children of Jerusalem tend to be those who focus on God's revelation and inspired Word, associated with Jerusalem as the center of Judeo-Christian religions. According to the Biblical record, King David captured Jerusalem from the Jebusites and made it his capital. It is known as the City of David and was the location of Solomon's Temple (later described as the First Temple), destroyed by the Babylonians but rebuilt some 70 years later after King Cyrus released the Jewish captives. It was in this Temple that Jesus was located by his parents (Luke 2: 46), tempted by Satan (Matthew 4:5; Luke 4:9), and where he turned over the tables of the moneychangers. Jerusalem is the city where Jesus was crucified and resurrected and the most holy city for Christians and Jews. In this metaphor the Children of Jerusalem are represented in Wesley's Quadrilateral under the banner of "Scripture."

Broadly speaking, today's theological debated regarding homosexuality is represented in the Children of Athens camp by leaders of the Methodist Federation for Social Action (MFSA), who advocate on a host of social gospel issues including full equality for the LGBTQ community. Good News leads the Children of Jerusalem Camp: Good News is a confessing movement within our denomination focused on evangelism and ministry who maintain that homosexuality is incompatible with Christian teaching. These two organizations tend to supply the rhetoric, resources and talking points for this divisive topic. The two groups are openly discussing and considering a split within the denomination, a separation that would at least end the theological debate and enable each side of this theological chasm to focus on its mission and ministry and end this seemingly interminable infighting.

When thinking about division over theological concepts, however, consider this:

Two hundred years ago Methodist Circuit Riders in the United States were discouraged from marriage. The life of a circuit rider was harsh and often short-lived and it was deemed that marriage was inappropriate for life on the frontier. But circuit riders were allowed to supplement their income with the sale of alcohol—a practice acceptable to Methodist leaders at the time (it is well known that John Wesley, while he was deeply opposed to the manufacture, sale and drinking of hard alcohol, enjoyed wine and beer and even published home brewing tips).

A hundred years later (and a hundred years ago now) the Methodist Church encouraged its preachers to marry. The Western Frontier had essentially closed, the nation was settled and the Methodist Church itself had become an established, mainline denomination. Married clergy, it was reasoned, were likely to attract settled couples and families to their churches and fuel the growth of the denomination. Meanwhile, Methodists were leaders in the Temperance Movement that led to Prohibition. Many Methodists a century ago signed pledges to abstain from alcohol for the remainder of their lives. It is funny how things changed, at least with respect to these two issues. The Methodist Church flipped 180° on the consumption of alcohol and whether clergy should be married. What issues will our denomination, if still in existence, be of a different opinions on one hundred years from now?

It is a common understanding that theologians in the Middle Ages discussed how many angels could stand (or dance) on the head of a pin. While this belief has been called into doubt in recent years, it serves as a warning and illustration for our times.

The Methodist Church has split multiple times in the past. Most notable among these divisions are these:

Church Name	Leader/Year	Reason
African Methodist Episcopal Church (AME)	Richard Allen: 1816	Denomination formed in response to American Methodists racial discrimination against African Americans.
Wesleyan Methodist Church	Orange Scott, La Roy Sutherland and J. Horton: 1841	Issues of slavery, church polity and the doctrine of holiness.

Methodist Episcopal Church, South	No single person led this schism but the inheritance of slaves by Bishop James Osgood Andrew led to the split in 1844	The issue of slavery split the Methodist Episcopal Church along northern and southern lines.
Free Methodist Church	A charismatic leader was the Rev. Benjamin Titus Roberts: 1860	The founding members of the Free Methodist Church, including Rev. Roberts, were expelled from the Methodist Episcopal Church over doctrinal and worship practices.
Salvation Army	William Booth: 1865	Booth believed the Methodist Church had lost its commitment to the poor.
Colored Methodist Episcopal Church	No specific leader can be identified with the formation of this denomination in 1870.	The Colored Methodist Episcopal Church, now known as the Christian Methodist Episcopal Church, separated from the Methodist Episcopal Church in the wake of the Civil War so that African American Methodists could establish and maintain their own polity.

Church of the Nazarene	Phineas Bresee and Joseph Pomeroy Widney: 1895	Theological differences with the Methodist Episcopal Church concerning the concept of "holiness" and focus on the Great Commission of Matthew 28:19.
Fire Baptized Holiness Church	Benjamin Hardin Irwin: 1895	Theological disputes with the Methodist Episcopal Church, primarily related to the understanding of sanctification.

CONCLUSION

The United Methodist Church is a church in decline. No one can disagree with this statement. Right now individuals and organizations are working on plans to split the UMC. They maintain that 30+ years of division are enough and that it is time for a divorce so that each faction can proceed with a unified theology and message.

Before we approach the seemingly inevitable vote of separation and division I pray that local church members, superintendents, bishops, delegates to annual, jurisdictional and General Conference will continue reading in order to consider an alternative to this pending, avoidable decision. I offer, in the following pages, this potential solution: let us "set aside" our theological differences and work together to serve the needs of orphans and vulnerable children. Working together for a common cause is, I believe, a better way.

CHAPTER II

....

Recipe for a Denomination in Decline:

John Wesley Redux

"If any want to become my followers, let them deny themselves
and take up their cross daily and follow me. For those who
want to save their lives will lose it, and those who lose their life
for my sake will save it. What does it profit them if they gain
the whole world, but lose or forfeit themselves?"
—LUKE 9: 23-25

O brethren, let us not still fall out by the way. I hope to see
you in heaven. And if I practice the religion above described,
you dare not say I shall go to hell. You cannot think so. None
can persuade you to it. Your own conscience tells you the con-
trary. Then if we cannot as yet think alike in all things, at least
we may love alike. Herein we cannot possible do amiss. For of
one point none can doubt a moment: God is love; and he that
dwelleth in love, dwelleth in God, and God in him [John 4:16].
—JOHN WESLEY,
A LETTER TO A ROMAN CATHOLIC, 1749

33

Jeremias and Naftal: Shaila not present for this photo

"I want to show you this. Three children are sitting under a tree. They are Jeremias (8), Shaila (6), and Naftal (5), siblings together at the Carolyn Belshe Orphanage (CBO) in Cambine, Mozambique. The younger two are crying and the older child is bravely, but barely, holding back tears. This is their third day at the orphanage; they arrived after a four-week journey that began with the death of their mother and included several nights with assorted neighbors and distant relatives, and other nights huddled under a bridge, clinging together against the African cool winter evening temperatures (mid-50° Fahrenheit). I met them during a VIM trip to Mozambique in 2006—they arrived at the orphanage while I was staying nearby. Their father had been a successful government leader, their mother a typical stay-at-home African mother who raised chickens, tended a modest vegetable plot, walked miles to get water, and cooked over an indoor, wood-fueled fire pit. The couple died from HIV/AIDS; the disease was transmitted to the father through a tainted blood donation he received several years earlier during otherwise routine surgery. The children ended up at this orphanage because their parents had been members of a local Methodist Church and had connections to the conference leadership."

I read somewhere that lost items usually turn up within three feet of where you thought that item was last placed. For instance, I generally leave my keys on a corner of my work desk. Some mornings the keys are missing and a frantic pursuit ensues. For the majority of times, however, I return to my desk and after shifting some papers or looking behind my books the missing keys are found. Lost items can often be found very close to where they are suppose to be.

In the same manner, the "lost" message of the UMC can be found by returning to the journal, sermons, publications, personal practices and worldview of John Wesley, founder of the Methodist Movement. Fortunately, the means for our success can be found by a return to our roots and heritage by re-visiting the ministry and message of Brother John, whose overriding mission was to be a faithful disciple of Jesus Christ in all that entails.

JOHN WESLEY AND THE METHODISTS

There was a time when the Methodist movement grew rapidly within the United States, with the church's primary mission, affirmed by John Wesley himself in the "Large" Minutes, with these words: "What may we reasonably believe to be God's design in raising up the Preachers called Methodists? A. To reform the nation and, in particular, the Church; to spread scriptural holiness over the land."

I misread this important Q & A passage for decades. For years I thought Wesley's focus was on **reforming the nation** [Great Britain and, by extension, the US Colonies] and spreading scriptural holiness over the [same] land (s).

For the past few years, however, I have been struck by Wesley's emphasis on **reforming "the Church."** The distinction is important—note Wesley's words: "What may we reasonably believe to be God's design in raising up the Preachers called Methodists? A. To reform the nation **and, in particular, the Church**; to spread scriptural holiness over the land." [Bold added]

John and Charles Wesley did desire, no doubt, to reform their nation and "spread scriptural holiness over the land." The Wesley brothers lived at the dawn of the Industrial Revolution in Great Britain where economic development was exaggerating income inequality. Simply put, the rich were getting richer and the poor, poorer. Governmental institutions were ill equipped to help those in need as a free market, *laisse – faire* economic system developed. The Wesley's devoted great resources of time, talent, gifts and service towards improving the human conditions of the poor while directing the people called Methodists to do the same.

A closer reading of this passage, however, confirms that the Wesley brothers were more focused on reforming **in particular, the Church**," over and above their work on reforming "the land." John and Charles Wesley were, like their father and older brother (both named Samuel), faithful priests of the Church of England. But John and Charles were convinced that their "Church" had strayed from its roots and the radical vision of its founder, Jesus Christ. They sought to reform, renew and transform the Church of England by returning to "scriptural holiness" based on the early church model as described in the New Testament. They sought to make their church more faithful and closer to the life and witness of Jesus Christ, from which they were convinced "the Church" had strayed.

Over the course of their careers John and Charles Wesley actually created "a church within a church:" they developed the theology, practices, polity, hymnal and preachers for the Methodist Movement within the overall organizational structure of the Church of England. It was this "reformed" movement, this "church within a church," the Wesley brothers believed, that would "spread scriptural holiness across the land:" it was this movement that would eventually develop into the independent Methodist Church.

The reformed, renewed, transformed and ideal church that the Wesley brothers sought to foster was based on their great knowledge of the Bible and personal conviction that their church did not meet their expectations of what the Church of Jesus Christ should look like. Their Biblical interpretation and beliefs grew out of decades of prayer, study and discussions: from this footing in faith and study they developed the blueprints and laid the foundation of our denomination.

The Wesleyan model church has a theology that places it squarely within the Protestant Camp. Their theological starting point is humanity's fall and corresponding doctrine of original sin that leads to death and eternal suffering. But God, through the sacrifice of Jesus Christ, offers humanity the gift of prevenient grace through which humans can "flee from the wrath to come." The path to heaven is through faith in Jesus Christ. Period.

From this starting point Wesley encouraged his people to participate in the ongoing means of grace: the two-pronged exercise through which the people called Methodist would grow in faith and knowledge of God *and* love of neighbor on the path towards perfection. The means of grace are 1) the works of piety and 2) the works of mercy. The works of piety and works of mercy were the practical means through which the Wesleyan Theology was grounded and manifest in the real world.

John Wesley had only one condition through which admission to a Methodist society could be obtained—individuals needed to express a desire to flee from the wrath to come. If an individual confessed to this request he or she was granted entrance into a society. To continue in a society, though, one needed to attend to the General Rules: 1) by doing no harm, and avoiding evil of every kind; 2) by doing good; and 3) by attending upon the ordinances of God. The General Rules were enforced through individual and corporate participation in the means of grace which included both the works of piety and the works of mercy, a two-stepped approach through which Christians grew in grace, knowledge and love of God and neighbor.

The works of piety included public and private prayer, study of scripture, confession and fasting, as well as praise and worship. **The works of mercy** are service to those in need, including feeding the hungry, clothing the naked, visiting the imprisoned, the sick, and the afflicted. Together, then, the works of piety and the works of mercy become the two legs on which humans walk into the eternal realm of God.

Wesley's linking of the works of mercy to the works of piety as the means of grace is clearly one of John's unique contributions to Christian theology and practice. (Rieger 2002:86) But what also needs to be mentioned is Wesley's preferential placement of the works of mercy *above* the works of piety. This can be clearly seen in his sermon *On Zeal*, dated 1781, when John was in his 78th year.

Developing a vision of what really matters in the Christian life, Wesley worked out a framework of four concentric circles. At the center is love, more precisely the double focus of love of God and love of neighbor. In the next circle to the center Wesley locates what he calls "holy tempers." ["holy tempers," defined by Wesley as the fruits of the spirit defined in Galatians 5, such as long suffering, gentleness, meekness, goodness, fidelity, temperance.] The next circle contains works of mercy and in the fourth circle are works of piety (the traditional means of grace). In the outermost circle Wesley locates the church. (Rieger 2002:86)

Wesley quotes in this sermon from Isaiah, Hosea and Matthew, each of who find fault with corporate worship when human needs are more pressing (for instance, Isaiah 1: 13, "Bring no more vain oblations," and Matthew, quoting Hosea: "God will have mercy and not sacrifice," Hosea 6:6; Matthew 9:13). God seeks justice and mercy, Wesley reminds us, above sacrifices and empty worship. This focus on the works of mercy is part of a greater Wesleyan theological transformation—that our service to those in need is not simply one sided wherein those with resources give to those without—but that those who give of their time, talents, gifts and service *also* receive as they themselves come in contact with the God of Jesus Christ. Grace is received through the works of piety, for sure, but just so (if not even more) when we serve the least, the last and the lost. In the same way that most humans have a dominant side (arm, leg), so too do the works of mercy hold the ascendant position of the stronger of the means of grace. In this way, "John prioritized works of mercy over works of piety." (Warner 2008:125)

Candido's Story, continued:

After much prayer and discussion the decision to adopt Candido and bring him to the US was made. Working with GBGM and church leaders, plans to adopt Candido moved smoothly. Approximately six months after I left Mozambique Candido had a passport, visa and ticket to the US. My good friend and GBGM missionary Lucille had taken care of the paperwork on that side of the ocean while I, my family and friends prayed and did what we could in Connecticut. Candido, pictured here playing with his cousin Griffin, arrived in the US knowing no English and having never experienced so many things we take for granted: running water (Candido never had a shower before his first one at our house in Connecticut), central heating and air conditioning, electricity, busses to school, cable TV and VCR's with movies at will, indoor kitchens with refrigerators, stoves and microwaves. He was overwhelmed and teary, missing his friends, but working hard to adjust.

A big concern was Candido's limited formal education, and his complete ignorance of our culture, customs and ways. He had no idea, for instance, of who Peter Pan or Pinocchio were, and was equally unaware of the existence of zoos and circuses. He knew nothing of dinosaurs, geography, math or science, and a steep learning curve was placed in his path.

Of even greater concern, of which I was ignorant, was his emotional health, which was impacted by both post-traumatic stress disorder and a severe case of reactive attachment disorder. It was not too long before Candido began acting out and becoming more and more violent. It was clear that he was having trouble adjusting to life in the United States.

JOHN WESLEY'S ECONOMIC PERSPECTIVE

John Wesley's economic perspective can best be described as radical. In multiple sermons (see, for example, "On Riches," "The Dangers of Riches," "On the Danger of Increasing Riches"), throughout his journal, in his exhortation to his preachers and in his personal activities he described and practiced how the increase of wealth led to a corresponding and correlated decline and death in faith and spirituality. Randy Maddox has summarized Wesley's thought through this four-fold approach:

1. Ultimately, everything belongs to God; 2) Resources are placed in our care to use as God sees fit; 3) God desires that we use these resources to meet our necessities (i.e. providing shelter and food for ourselves and dependents), and then to help others in need; thus, 4) Spending resources on luxuries for ourselves while others remain in need is robbing God. (Maddox 2002:62)

Hear Wesley in his own words:

> Surely you cannot be ignorant, that the sinfulness of fine apparel lies chiefly in the expensiveness: In that it is robbing God and the poor; it is defrauding the fatherless and the widow; it is wasting the food of the hungry, and withholding his raiment from the naked to consume it on our own lusts. (A Farther Appeal, 1745, Wesley 1987a:256)

> The more you lay out on your own apparel, the less you have left to clothe the naked, to feed the hungry, to lodge the strangers, to relieve those that are sick and in prison, and to lessen the numberless afflictions to which we are exposed in this vale of tears . . . . Every shilling which you save from your own apparel, you may expend in clothing

the naked, and relieving the various necessities of the poor, whom ye "have always with you." Therefore, every shilling which you needlessly spend on your own apparel is, in effect, stolen from God and the poor! (On Dress, 1786, Wesley 1986a:254)

Not that money is an evil of itself: It is applicable to good as well as bad purposes. But, nevertheless, it is an undoubted truth, that "the love of money is the root of all evil;" and also, that the possession of riches naturally breeds the love of them. (Mystery of Iniquity, 1783, Wesley 1985c:468)

Whoever has sufficient food to eat and raiment to put on, with a place where to lay his head, and something over, is rich. (Danger of Riches, 1772, Wesley 1986b:230)

They have read or heard these words [about laying up treasure] an hundred times, and yet never suspect that they are themselves condemned thereby, and more than by those which forbid parents to offer up their own sons or daughters unto Moloch. *(Sermon on the Mount, VIII, 1748, Wesley 1984b:618)*

This affording to rob God is the very cant of hell. Do not you know that God entrusted you with that money (above what buys necessaries for your family) to feed the hungry, to clothe the naked, to help the stranger, the widow, the fatherless; and, indeed, as far as it will go to relieve the wants of all mankind. (Danger of Increasing Riches, 1790, Wesley 1987e:184)

These quotes are but a brief sampling and example of the extensive Wesleyan writings that reflect his strong and literal understanding of Biblical texts in regard to possessions and the dangers and snares of wealth. Speaking plainly and boldly to his people, Wesley laid out a counter-cultural personal economic model based on scriptural passages from the Old and New Testaments where the building of God's kingdom is accomplished through grace, peace, mercy and love. All Wesleyan readers must be aware that this is our heritage.

But more than just preach these words, John Wesley lived this lifestyle. Every indication is that although he was a person of great substance who could have amassed extensive personal wealth, he consistently gave away virtually everything he earned, never personally owning more than £10 at any time. He learned while living at Oxford that he could live on £30 per year (about $5,000 in 2015—this figure does not include housing), and lived on that amount the rest of his life despite earning as much as £1500 ($250,000) some years. What did Wesley do with the extra £1470 he earned those years, and the surplus income he obtained other years? He saved it and, by not spending in on items he considered nonessential, was able to give it to the poor. Wesley described his personal approach in *An Earnest Appeal to Men of Reason and Religion*, published in 1744, wherein he wrote:

> Food and raiment I have; such food as I choose to eat, and
> such raiment as I choose to put on. I have a place where to
> lay my head. I have what is needful for life and godliness.
> And I apprehend this is all the world can afford. The kings
> of the earth can give me no more. For as to gold and silver I
> count it dung and dross; I trample it under my feet. I (yet
> not I, but the grace of God that is in me) esteem it just as
> the mire in the streets. I desire it not; I seek it not; I only fear
> lest any of it should cleave to me, and I should not be able to
> shake it off before my spirit returns to God. It must indeed

pass through my hands; but I will take care (God being my helper) that the mammon of unrighteousness shall only pass through; it shall not rest there. None of the accursed thing shall be found in my tents when the Lord calleth me hence. And hear ye this, all you who have discovered the treasures which I am to leave behind me: If I leave behind me ten pounds, (above my debts, and my books, or what may happen to be due on account of them,) you and all mankind bear witness against me, that I lived and died a thief and a robber. (Wesley 1987b:87 – 88)

A decade later, gravely sick from tuberculosis and fearing his death, John wrote his own epitaph: "Here lieth the body of John Wesley, a brand, not once only, plucked out of the fire; he died of a consumption in the fifty-first year of his age, leaving (after his debts were paid) not ten pounds behind him, praying—God be merciful to me an unprofitable servant." (Journal, Nov. 1753, Wesley 1991a:482) Fortunately for John *and* for us, Wesley recovered from this illness and lived another three decades plus, but kept his beliefs and practices on personal wealth accumulation steady. Fast-forward another decade after his near-death illness and we find this warning to his societies:

I gave all our brethren a solemn warning not to love the world, or the things of the world. This is one way whereby Satan will surely endeavour to overthrow the present work of God. Riches swiftly increase on many Methodists, so called: What, but the mighty power of God, can hinder their setting their hearts upon them? And if so, the life of God vanishes away. (Journal, July 11, 1764, Wesley 1992:477)

One of John Wesley's most quoted phrases is this: "Earn all you can, save all you can, give all you can." (Wesley 1987c:91) Many Americans are pretty good at the first of these imperatives, but not so much on the next two. Earn all you can, save all you can, however, is not a recipe for a prosperity gospel worldview but instead practical instructions so that you can *give* more aid to those in need. Wesley could not have been clearer on this topic: "If you have any desire to escape the damnation of hell, give all you can; otherwise I can have no more hope of your salvation, than of that of Judas Iscariot." (Causes of the Inefficacy of Christians, 1789, Wesley 1987c:96)

PERSONAL PRACTICES

It is clear that John Wesley's had a profound sense of social justice: it is not clear where this attitude was created, although it is likely that he developed it at an early age. His father, of course, was a Church of England cleric who served as the priest in Epworth, England, for 40 years. His wife, Susanna, raised the children and gave them a solid education in languages, religion and Bible. For her labors she earned the name "Mother of Methodism."

When John was a young boy of five the rectory where he and his family lived caught on fire: it was the cold night of February 9, 1709. It is possible the fire was set by one of his father's enemies—to this day no one knows how the fire started. However, years later John wrote in his diary: "The next day, as he [here John is writing about his father] was walking in the garden and surveying the ruins of the house, he picked up part of a leaf of his polyglot Bible, on which just these words were legible, *Vade; yende mnia quae habes, et attolle crucem, et sequere Me.* "Go; sell all that thou hast; and take up thy cross, and follow Me."

This story, otherwise undocumented but likely true—at least in Wesley's memory—is instructive if we are to understand John Wesley. Wesley did not sell *all* that he owned, but he *intentionally* never owned much. Further, "it is clear that his own life-style was governed by the attempt to live without the snare of possessions, to give all to the poor, and so to follow the precepts of the gospel as he understood them." (Jennings 1990:120) From his early years at Oxford "Wesley demonstrated a concern for the widows, orphans, and prisoners of the city." (Heitzenrater 2002:25) This life-style is evidenced in several letters to his brother written while he was a student at Oxford: he described, in these letters how, by letting his hair grow long, he was able to save money and give to the poor. (Wesley 1987d:222 & 320) Years later he decided to give up tea and use the savings (earn all you can, **save** all you can by not spending on items like tea that are non-essentials, give all you can) for the poor, as he wrote: "I will compute this day what I have expended in tea, weekly or yearly. I will immediately enter on cheaper food: And whatever is saved hereby, I will put into the poor-box weekly, to feed the hungry, and to clothe the naked." (Wesley 1830:Vol. XI, p. 500)

John Wesley gave both personally, from his own pockets to those who begged from him (despite this being against the law in England at the time) (Heitzenrater 2002:31), and institutionally through the movement he established. "As early as 1742, Methodist people were expected to give a penny a week to their class leader in support of the beneficent programs of the connection. Captain Foy, a lay leader in Bristol, suggested that if a poor person could not meet that expectation, the class leader should make up the difference. He backed up his suggestion by volunteering to assume responsibility for twelve of the poorest people in the society." (Heitzenrater 2002:32)

Wesley established a practice of personally visiting the sick and poor and believed that these experiences helped his growth in faith, service, love and grace, writing "Yet I find time to visit the sick and the poor; and I must do it, if I believe the Bible." (Letter, to Miss March, 12/10/1777 Wesley 1777) Visiting the sick, the poor, the imprisoned were, in Wesley's mind, the works of mercy and an essential component of the means of grace, to be considered even more important than the works of piety such as private and public prayer, Bible study and / or the sacraments itself. (Wesley 1984a:313) We visit the poor, Wesley maintained, not just for the benefit of the poor but, just as essential, for ours as well. He wrote often of his experiences visiting the poor, as in this account:

> On Friday and Saturday, I visited as many [of the poor] as
> I could. I found some in their cells underground; others in
> their garrets, half-starved both with cold and hunger, added
> to weakness and pain . . . .If you saw these things with your
> own eyes, could you lay out money in ornaments or super-
> fluities? (Journal, February 9 - 10, 1753, Wesley 1991b:445)

Finally, consider this next journal entry from Mr. Wesley when, at the age
of 82, he walked the streets of London to collect funds for the poor:

> At this season [Christmas] we usually distribute coals and
> bread among the poor of the society [of London]. But I now
> considered, they wanted clothes, as well as food. So on this,
> and the four following days, I walked through the town, and
> begged two hundred pounds, in order to clothe them that
> needed it most. But it was hard work, as some of the streets
> were filled with melting snow, which often lay ankle deep;
> so that my feet were steeped in snow-water nearly from
> morning till evening. I held it out pretty well till Saturday
> evening I was laid up with a violent flux which increased ev-
> ery hour, till six in the morning Dr. Whitehead called upon
> me" (Journal, January 4, 1785, Wesley 1995:340)

Wesley not only personally earned all he could, saved all he could, gave all
he could, he also established within his societies that its members would
regularly collect for the poor, and begged from others so that he could give
their resources to the poor. He was also a visionary leader, prescient in setting up free health clinics, forming cottage industries / collectives and establishing micro-loan programs for the poor. He organized for the poor so
that they would be able to meet their own needs. Again, in his own words:

> I mentioned to the society my design of giving physic to the
> poor. About thirty came the next day, and in three weeks
> about three hundred. This we continued for several years,
> till, the number of patience still increasing, the expense was

greater than we could bear. Meantime, through the blessing of God, many who had been ill for months of years, were restored to perfect health. (Journal, Nov. 25, 1746, Wesley 1992:150–151)

Our aim was, with as little expense as possible, to keep them at once from want and from idleness: in order to which, we took twelve of the poorest, and a teacher, into the society-room, where they were employed for four months, till spring came on, in carding and spinning of cotton: And the design answered: They were employed and maintained with very little more than the produce of their own labour. (Journal, Nov. 25, 1740, Wesley 1990:173)

I made a public collecting towards a lending stock for the poor. Our rule is, to lend only twenty-shillings at once, which is repaid weekly within three months. I began this about a year and a half ago [1746]: Thirty pounds sixteen shillings were then collected; and of this, no less than two hundred and fifty-five persons have been relieved in eighteen months. (Journal, Jan. 17, 1748, Wesley 1991a:204)

It can be said that John Wesley had a preferential love of the poor, and established the institutional discipline of caring for the poor not only for the poor themselves, but because of the benefit it has on those who are in positions to help: "Go and see the poor and sick in their own poor little hovels. Take up your cross, woman! Remember the faith! Jesus went before you, and will go with you. Put off the gentlewoman: You bear a higher character. You are an heir of God, and joint heir with Christ!" (Letter to a Member of the Society, June 9, 1775, Wesley 1850:Vol. VI, 782)

Here is the key: "In visiting the marginalized, we invite them to transform us, to transform our hearts, to transform our understanding, to transform us into instruments of the divine mercy and justice." (Jennings 1990:57–58) Our service to those in need is not solely for their benefit: we too receive when we give—and often we benefit more than those we seek to serve.

John Wesley's economic worldview, based on his understanding of scripture and his personal spirituality, is radical. It is simultaneously inspiring and challenging, especially to those of us raised within the US where the cultural message is one of unabated consumer consumption, unfettered capitalism and a burning desire to make and then spend money on ourselves in order to enjoy a more and more luxurious lifestyle. When Americans get a raise, generally speaking, it means nicer clothing, a bigger home, more expensive cars, exotic vacations, better foods, etc. and not necessarily more money to be saved so that it can then be given away.

Wesley's economic worldview stands in stark contrast to the so-called prosperity gospel, aka prosperity theology or the gospel of success. The prosperity gospel is the belief that financial blessings and success are the will of God for Christians, and that faith and donations to Christian ministries will lead to an increase in one's material wealth. It is derived, in part, from Calvinism, our Puritan ancestors, who were faced with the problem of succession and working with a theology that made it impossible to determine who would be saved and who would be damned. They created a formula to choose leaders from "those God has prospered." And, ironically, whose theology did John Wesley find more distasteful than any other with the possible exception of Roman Catholicism? John Calvin.

The prosperity gospel message has flourished within the US in correlation to our great wealth: the US is the richest nation in the history of the world and the nation that gave birth to this non-traditional interpretation of the Biblical message. H. R. Niebuhr enlightened us years ago of how religion is influenced / compromised by the culture in which it is found in his brilliant work, *Christ and Culture* (Niebuhr 1956), and we can easily witness the corrupting power of money within this nation and understand how the American culture has worked its way into our denomination.

The US was founded, in part, on a search for wealth and prosperity. While we think of the Puritan's search for religious freedom they were also shrewd business leaders intent on material prosperity. Jamestown, the first English-speaking settlement in North America, was funded by a group of entrepreneurs seeking economic opportunities. Promises of gold and silver were soon replaced with more realistic goals: John Rolfe found great success planting tobacco from which he became prosperous and wealthy. The shareholders of the Virginia Company thereafter realized some profitability as the colony became more efficient and productive.

The "American Dream" is essentially a set of ideals and hopes that include freedom and the opportunity for material prosperity and success, with upward social mobility obtained via hard work and determination. Persons from around the world yearn to come to the US to participate in our material wealth, a seemingly inherent conflict for followers of Jesus Christ who warned us again and again of the dangers of wealth and told us "It will be hard for a rich person to enter the kingdom of heaven. Again I tell you, it is easier for a camel to go through the eye of a needle than for someone who is rich to enter the kingdom of God." (Matthew 19: 23-24) Contrast that with this quintessential quote from US President Calvin Coolidge: "The business of the American people is business."

The merger of US corporations and religion was truly consummated in the 1930's in response to the Great Depression and FDR's New Deal. Corporations and "Wall Street Greed" had been blamed for the financial collapse and hence were on the defensive. There was great angst among the business leaders about the threat posed by socialism / Bolshevism and the continuing gains of the labor movement. To fight back, corporations laid out "an inspired public relations offensive that cast capitalism as the handmaiden of Christianity. The two had been described as soul mates before, but in this campaign they were wedded in pointed opposition to the 'creeping socialism' of the New Deal." (Kruse 2015) Throughout the 1930's and 1940's corporate leaders intentionally sought to link Christianity with free market business, and shrewdly hired clergy to be their PR agents. The Rev. James W. Fifield, aka "the 13th Apostle of Big Business" and "Saint Paul of the Prosperous," (Kruse 2015) was one of the early leaders of this movement. Rev. Fifield said: reading the Bible is "like eating fish—we take the bones out to enjoy the meal. All parts are not of equal value." (Kruse 2015) He rejected New Testament writings warning about the dangers of wealth and instead connected Christianity and capitalism against FDR's "pagan statism."

Many TV evangelists are associated with prosperity gospel, including the widely successful and contemporary speaker and author Joel Olsteen. But the most influential religious leader of this movement was the Rev. Billy Graham, who supported corporate interests so fervently that he was dubbed "The Big Business evangelist." "'The Garden of Eden,' he informed revival attendees, 'was a paradise with 'no union dues, no labor leaders, no snakes, no disease.' In the same spirit, he denounced all 'governments restrictions' in economic affairs, which he invariably attacked as socialism." (Kruse 2015)

Many UMC pastors themselves preach, or at the least practice, a version of prosperity gospel. We seek larger congregations with higher steeples and bigger salaries. We complain about our parsonages when billions of persons around the planet live in substandard housing and would be over joyed to live in these homes. We participate in pension programs, save for retirement and hope to live in comfort with an abundance of food and other material benefits. UMC bishops receive an annual salary north of $141,000, plus housing, plus benefits, plus expenses, and superintendents are compensated at approximately 50 percent of this amount. I know clergy in large congregations who receive salaries higher than bishops. These salaries are not, by US standards, excessive, especially when we consider the background of executive compensation in general within the US. But these salaries do point out how far we have come from the thinking and practices of John Wesley.

Of course, Wesley would not be against high salaries in and of themselves. His phrase, "Earn all you can, save all you can, give all you can" indicates that our earning power is not the issue: instead, we struggle with the second two imperatives.

Meanwhile, the affluence of many United Methodist Church members in the US has paralleled and, in some cases, exceeded that of clergy. I had a church member who was very successful: his company, of which he was the founder and CEO, owned a private jet that he used for business and personal trips. Another successful couple remodeled their kitchen to the tune of $75,000, while another couple built a $200,000 addition to their home for "extra space." I had in one church I served a UMC couple who own a multi-million dollar home in Darien, CT, and another in the Hamptons. Each of the fore mentioned couples give less than $2,000 to their church. In each church where I served and, as far as I can tell, in every church where I have been invited to speak, there is at least one church family with wealth, sometimes great wealth, and these wealthy members seem, generally speaking, to be reluctant to part with their money.

The UMC also has access to political power. Hillary Clinton is a life-long member of our denomination, and she and her husband have attended UMC services for decades. George and Barbara Bush are also UMC members. Rush Limbaugh is a United Methodist, as are Dick Cheney and John Edwards.

I spoke recently at a church whose conference has a Foundation with over $60 million. In speaking with the Chief Executive Officer, I learned that many other conferences Foundations have more or less the same amounts within their portfolios. His goal was to grow his Foundation to the $100 million level, from which the Foundation would be able to generate $5 million per year, aka 5% or half a tithe, for mission work.

Few of us live up to the standards John Wesley outlined and lived and we can all do better. Recognizing the toxicity and corrupting nature of the culture in which we live, however, is the first step towards repentance and conversion. If we, as a denomination, were to take this adage from John Wesley seriously, "Earn all you can, save all you can, give all you can," we could change the lives of millions of OVC and simultaneously change our own lives and that of our denomination.

ECUMENICAL SPIRIT

John Benjamin Wesley (I bet most readers never knew John's middle name) must have been as convinced that his beliefs, theology, practices and interpretation of the Bible were as accurate as anyone else. With incredible organizational skills and undaunted enthusiasm and courage he established the Methodist movement within the Church of England that would eventually split off and create the Methodist Movement that today claims over 80 million followers within the World Methodist Council. He established our Doctrinal Standards and General Rules, published pamphlets, books, sermons and hymnals, organized and eventually ordained preachers, built meeting houses and held conferences through which his theology and vision were communicated and statistical information recorded. John Wesley traveled the length and breath of Great Britain, preached thousands of sermons, met countless individuals and left an incredible legacy. He was a remarkable person noted as one of the most significant men of the 18th Century.

But John Wesley also knew that, on any particular issue, he might be wrong.

In one of his most fascinating sermons, but in multiple other settings, Wesley stressed "In essentials, unity; in nonessentials, liberty; and in all things, charity." (Alexander 2012:51) That noted sermon is "Catholic Spirit," delivered in 1750 and based on the text from 2 Kings 10: 15. "And when he was departed thence, he lighted on Jehonadab the son of Rechab coming to meet him: and he saluted him and said to him, 'Is thine heart right as my heart is with thy heart?' And Jehonadab answered, 'It is.' 'If it be, give me thine hand.'"

It is within this sermon that Wesley delivers these critical lines: "Though we cannot think alike, may we not love alike? May we not be of one heart, though we are not of one opinion? Without all doubt, we may. Herein all the children of God may unite, notwithstanding these smaller differences." (Wesley 1985a:82) He continues, "Nay, farther: although every man necessarily believes that every particular opinion which he holds is true (for to believe any opinion is not true, is the same thing as not to hold it); yet can no man be assured that all of his own opinions, taken together, are true . . . . He knows, in the general, that he himself is mistaken; although in what particulars he mistakes, he does not, perhaps he cannot, know." (Catholic Spirit, 1750, Wesley 1985a:83–84)

A few paragraphs later Wesley is equally brilliant and on point. He chooses to discuss manners and modes of worship and differences in church government. He asks if his listeners receive the sacrament of communion in the same manner as he, and whether or not they observe baptism in the same way, with the same age of those to be baptized? He concludes: "Let all these things stand by: we will talk of them, if need be, at a more convenient season; my only question at present is this, 'Is thine heart right, as my heart is with thy heart?'" (Catholic Spirit, 1750, Wesley 1985a:90)

John Wesley, who was born, raised, educated and ordained within the Church of England, held a "high church" perspective of how worship was to be conducted and observed. But he was practical enough to take up field preaching despite what he had been taught and believed: that it was vile and inappropriate. He was wise enough to know that the manner in which we worship, like so many other nonessential beliefs and practices we hold, are not critically important. What is foremost is where you heart is: and if you heart is in the right place, it is possible and even for the best to put aside insignificant differences and serve together.

It is well known that John Wesley and George Whitefield had a falling out over the theological concept of predestination. Once best friends, colleagues, priests and members of the Holy Club at Oxford, Whitefield and Wesley stood on different sides of this theological chasm. They conducted a public debate on this topic and no doubt created much pain and sorrow for each other. But, in time, they reached an important stage, the willingness to agree to disagree. It is this decision, I believe, where Wesley was at his best. And it was this decision, I believe, that opened the path through which George Whitefield and John Wesley were able to forge a partnership that resulted in the Great Awakening of the 18th Century. Their friendship intact, mission field served, conversion of souls and organizational structure of the Methodist movement as priorities, George Whitefield and John Wesley were able to set aside their different theological positions on pre-destination and take each others hands in service. It was this agreement to disagree that would lead to John's delivery of George Whitefield's eulogy when the charismatic preacher / evangelist / co-leader of the Great Awakening / friend died in 1770.

CONCLUSION

The United Methodist Church is a denomination in decline: given the current statistical and demographic trends, our denomination is well on the path towards irrelevancy and will reach this status by mid-century despite the best efforts of a few inspiring, charismatic clergy and laity sprinkled across the nation in various conferences and locations. Our *connexion* within the US has lost members *every single year* since its creation in 1968. Denominational quarreling, theological infighting and special interest groups vying for "power" have left the United Methodist Church family deeply divided and on bad terms internally. Within another generation our denomination will cease to exist in any significant manner unless these passionate forces are turned into a more positive direction.

And yet there is hope. Our hope lies in and through a return to our heritage, roots and foundation that were established by John Wesley some 250 years ago. His theological framework, economic perspective, personal practices and ecumenical spirit provide the blueprints in which we can revive our dying denomination and, at the same time, serve those in need. While we may not have in our time great numbers of individuals who are eager to "flee from the wrath to come," we still have millions of spiritually thirsty individuals searching for something worthwhile in which to give of themselves. John Wesley gave us the prescription to cure the disease of decline: we only must return to the source.

The seeds for our revival and re-birth lay within.

CHAPTER III

Methodists and Orphans

Blessed be the God and Father of our Lord Jesus Christ,
the Father of mercies and the God of all consolation, who
consoles us in all our affliction, so that we may be able to
console those who are in any affliction with the consola-
tion with which we ourselves are consoled by God.
—2 CORINTHIANS 1: 3 - 4

What is your heart made of? Is there no such principle
as Compassion there? Do you never feel another's pain?
Have you no Sympathy? No sense of human woe? No
pity for the miserable?
—JOHN WESLEY,
THOUGHTS ON SLAVERY 1774

The *2012 Book of Discipline* of the United Methodist Church does not include one mention of the word "orphan" within its 800+ pages. This is not necessarily surprising given that *The Book of Discipline* is primarily a book of the rules, doctrines and polity of the denomination. It is, however, somewhat disappointing given the amount of space *The Discipline* gives to our church's history, doctrinal standards, theological task, ministry and social principles.

I want to show you this. Hardi, Shamal, and Bahman are three children living in Halbja, Iraq. They are best friends-fourteen years old-living with their mothers because their dads were killed in different conflicts since the US-led invasion of Iraq in March 2003. I met them while leading a Foundation 4 Orphans event at a community center in Halabja in 2013. At the time I was serving as a visiting professor at the University of Human Development in Sulaymaniyah, about 60 miles from Halabja. Halabja is the location where Saddam Hussein's forces unleashed a devastating chemical attack against the civilian population on March 25, 1989. Hardi, Shamal, and Bahman are Kurds-the largest ethnic group in the world without their own nation. Currently they are citizens of Iraq, but in their minds, hopefully one day they will be citizens of a "yet to come into existence" Kurdistan. Hardi and Shamal's fathers were killed while serving in the Iraqi Army under Saddam Hussein, fighting against the US-led forces while simultaneously seeking a way to desert and get back to their families. Like many Kurdish men, Hardi and Shamal's fathers were draftees, forced to serve in the army while hating Saddam and the policies he represented. Bahman's father was killed fighting "insurgents," the precursors to ISIS, in 2012, fighting under the flag of the Kurdish Regional Government."

The 2012 Book of Resolutions of the United Methodist Church mentions the word "orphan" or "orphans" eight times in its 1000+ pages. Readers will note that with the exception of Resolution 6081 on "African Reconstruction and Development," all other references to the word "orphan" or "orphans" are scriptural quotes chosen almost robotically in efforts to find Biblical support to care for disadvantaged individuals or groups, none of which has any relationship to orphans.

☐ Page 546: Resolution 4052 *"Economic Justice for a New Millennium."* The first two mentions of the word "orphan" are found together in the section titled Biblical / Theological Background. "Christ teaches that faith requires action for social and spiritual well-being and especially care for the poor and the oppressed. The early church understood that all were to share all that they had and especially care for widows and **orphans** (Act 2:44 – 45; 2 Corinthians 8:13 – 15). Israel's early law codes required persons to meet human needs and guarantee basic economic and legal rights: food (Leviticus 19:9-10; Deuteronomy 23: 21-22; 24:19-22), clothing (Exodus 26- 27), just business dealings (Deuteronomy 25: 13-16), and access to just juridical process (Exodus 23: 6-8). Special concern is expressed for the marginalized in society; the poor (Exodus 23:6; Deuteronomy 15:7-11), the disabled (Mark 2:1-12), the stranger (Exodus 22:21-24; 23:9), the immigrant (Deuteronomy 10:19), the widow and the **orphan** (Deuteronomy 24:19-22)."

☐ Page 576: Resolution 4061 "Enabling Financial Support for Domestic Programs." "Our Christina faith has always compelled us to carry special concern for all people living in poverty, from Deuteronomy's commands to care for the widows and **orphans** to Jesus' shocking revelation that we are caring for him when we care for the "least of these" in our midst (Matthew 25)."

☐ Page 609: Resolution 4135 "Rights of Workers," and under the Biblical Theological Background we find this sentence: "The Book of Acts describes an early Christian community that shared its goods with one another; and throughout both Testaments,

God's people are urged to give special concern for widows, **orphans**, and immigrants."

☐ Page 682: Resolution 5083 refers to the "Rights to Privacy." Again, under the Theological Statement we read this sentence: "The prophets of Israel denounced the repression of the poor, the widow, **orphans**, and others of their society, and our Lord's ministry began with the announced purpose to set at liberty the poor and disadvantaged."

☐ Page 785: Resolution 6081 "African Reconstruction and Development." Under paragraph 7: continue and further develop the General Board of Global Ministries' commitment to health care in Africa through comprehensive, community-based health care, recognizing the role that poverty and poor sanitation play in the spread of communicable diseases across the continent; the collapse of the health-care systems in many countries; and the ineffectiveness of total reliance on institutional medical models. Support the revitalization of mission hospitals as critical adjuncts to community-based care. Support AIDS prevention training through the African Churches, AIDS **orphan** trusts, prevention of mother to child transmission of HIV and equipped and informed home care for terminally ill family members;

☐ Pages 876 and 877: Resolution 6147 "The Abolition of Torture." Here a verse from the Biblical Prophet Isaiah is quoted twice: "The biblical mandate is clear. It is not enough to cease evil. It is imperative to 'learn to do good. Seek justice: help the oppressed; defend the **orphan**; plead for the widow' (Isaiah 1:17)."

Seven of the eight times the word "orphan" or "orphans" is mentioned in *The Book of Resolutions* are in generic statements regarding how Christians are to act with mercy towards traditionally deprived and underprivileged groups. The only direct reference to helping orphans is in Resolution 6081: "African Reconstruction and Development," where the support of orphans from AIDS are mentioned and the establishment of orphan trusts is encouraged. Like *The Book of Discipline* (2012), *The Book of Resolutions* (2012) does not list the word "orphan" in its Table of Contents or Index.

The lack of attention given to orphans in these two defining books of the UMC is telling. To be sure, there are individuals, congregations, districts, conferences, GBGM programs and missionaries that work directly with orphans—at home and abroad—but the institutional church itself is, in general, AWOL in this important mission field. I know this personally after a futile period of 18 months in which I drove the length and breath of this nation seeking support for my work with orphans and vulnerable children. Feeling called to this ministry, I used my contacts to get meetings with church leaders across the nation. I was rebuffed by bishops and by members of the Connectional Table, by multiple denominational boards and agencies leaders, and by local pastors and local churches, big and small, rural and urban, liberal and conservative.

This MIA status of our denomination in the orphan field is disconcerting. It is disconcerting, in part, given the number of Biblical passages that implore us to serve the needs of orphans. It is equally disconcerting, given John Wesley's emphasis on works of mercy—in general—and specifically in his references to, direct work with and encouragement of others to serve the needs of orphans. Given that the Bible commands us thirty separate times to care for orphans, and that John Wesley both set up orphanages and encouraged the people called Methodist to do the same, this question needs to be asked: Why is the UMC doing so little in this field?

BIBLICAL TEXTS

Thirty times the Bible instructs its readers to care for orphans. The texts are so clear, direct and forceful that I have decided to include them here (all texts from NRSV):

☐ Exodus 22: 22-24

You shall not abuse any widow or orphan. If you do abuse them, when they cry out to me, I will surely heed their cry; my wrath will burn, and I will kill you with the sword, and your wives shall become widows and your children orphans.

☐ Deuteronomy 10:18-20

Who executes justice for the orphan and the widow, and who loves the strangers, providing them food and clothing. You shall also love the stranger, for you were strangers in the land of Egypt. You shall fear the Lord your God; him alone you shall worship; to him you shall hold fast, and by his name you shall swear.

☐ Deuteronomy 14:28-29

Every third year you shall bring out the full tithe of your produce for that year, and store it within your towns; the Levites, because they have no allotment or inheritance with you, as well as the resident aliens, the orphans, and the widows in your towns, may come and eat their fill so that the Lord your God may bless you in all the work that you undertake.

☐ Deuteronomy 24: 17-22

You shall not deprive a resident alien or an orphan of justice; you shall not take a widow's garment in pledge. Remember that you were a slave in Egypt and the Lord your God redeemed you from there; therefore I command you to do this. When you reap your harvest in your field and forget a sheaf in the field, you shall not go back to get it; it shall be left for the alien, the orphan, and the widow, so that the Lord your God may bless you in all your undertakings. When you beat your olive trees, do not strip what is left; it shall be for the alien, the orphan, and the widow. When you gather the grapes of your vineyard, do not glean what is left; it shall be for the alien, the orphan, and the widow. Remember that you were a slave in the land of Egypt; therefore I am commanding you to do this.

☐ Deuteronomy 26: 12-13

When you have finished paying all the tithe of your produce in the third year (which is the year of the tithe), giving it to the Levites, the aliens, the orphans, and the widows, so that they may eat their fill within your towns, then you shall say before the Lord your God: "I have removed the sacred portion from the house, and I have given it to the Levites, the resident aliens, the orphans, and the widows, in accordance with your entire commandment that you commanded me; I have neither transgressed nor forgotten any of your commandments.

☐ Deuteronomy 27:19

"Cursed be anyone who deprives the alien, the orphan, and the widow of justice." All the people shall say, "Amen!"

☐ Job 6:27

You would even cast lots over the orphan, and bargain over your friend.

☐ Job 29: 12-13

Because I delivered the poor who cried, and the orphan who had no helper. The blessing of the wretched came upon me, and I caused the widow's heart to sing for joy.

☐ Psalms 10:14

But you do see! Indeed you note trouble and grief, that you may take it into your hands; the helpless commit themselves to you; you have been the helper of the orphan.

☐ Psalm 68:5

Father of orphans and protector of widows is God in his holy habitation.

☐ Psalm 82:3:
Give justice to the weak and the orphan; maintain the right of the lowly and the destitute.

☐ Psalms 94: 4-7
They pour out their arrogant words; all the evildoers boast. They crush your people, O Lord, and afflict your heritage. They kill the widow and the stranger, they murder the orphan, and they say, "The Lord does not see; the God of Jacob does not perceive.

☐ Psalm 146:9
The Lord watches over the strangers; he upholds the orphan and the widow, but the way of the wicked he brings to ruin.

☐ Proverbs 23: 10 – 11
Do not remove an ancient landmark or encroach on the fields of orphans, for their redeemer is strong; he will plead their cause against you.

☐ Isaiah 1:17
Learn to do good; seek justice, rescue the oppressed, defend the orphan, plead for the widow.

☐ Isaiah 1:21-23
How the faithful city has become a whore! She that was full of justice, righteousness lodged in her—but now murderers! Your silver has become dross, your wine is mixed with water. Your princes are rebels and companions of thieves. Everyone loves a bribe and runs after gifts. They do not defend the orphan, and the widow's cause does not come before them.

☐ Isaiah 10:1-4
Ah, you who make iniquitous decrees, who write oppressive statutes, to turn aside the needy from justice and to rob the poor of my people of their right, that widows may be your spoil, and that you may make the orphans your prey! What will you do on the day of punishment, in the calamity that will come from

far away? To whom will you flee for help, and where will you leave your wealth, so as not to crouch among the prisoners or fall among the slain? For all this his anger has not turned away; his hand is stretched out still.

☐ Jeremiah 5:28

They have grown fat and sleek. They know no limits in deeds of wickedness; they do not judge with justice the cause of the orphan, to make it prosper, and they do not defend the rights of the needy.

☐ Jeremiah 7:5-7

For if you truly amend your ways and your doings, if you truly act justly one with another, if you do not oppress the alien, the orphan, and the widow, or shed innocent blood in this place, and if you do not go after other gods to your own hurt, then I will dwell with you in this place, in the land that I gave of old to your ancestors forever and ever.

☐ Jeremiah 22:3-5

Thus says the Lord: Act with justice and righteousness, and deliver from the hand of the oppressor anyone who has been robbed. And do no wrong or violence to the alien, the orphan, and the widow, or shed innocent blood in this place. For if you will indeed obey this word, then through the gates of this house shall enter kings who sit on the throne of David, riding in chariots and on horses, they, and their servants, and their people. But if you will not heed these words, I swear by myself, says the Lord, that this house shall become a desolation.

☐ Jeremiah 49:11

Leave your orphans, I will keep them alive; and let your widows trust in me.

☐ Hosea 14:3

Assyria shall not save us; we will not ride upon horses; we will say no more, 'Our God,' to the work of our hands. In you the orphan finds mercy."

☐ Zechariah 7:10

Do not oppress the widow, the orphan, the alien, or the poor; and do not devise evil in your hearts against one another.

☐ Ezekiel 22:7

Father and mother are treated with contempt in you; the alien residing within you suffers extortion; the orphan and the widow are wronged in you.

☐ Malachi 3:5

Then I will draw near to you for judgment; I will be swift to bear witness against the sorcerers, against the adulterers, against those who swear falsely, against those who oppress the hired workers in their wages, the widow and the orphan, against those who thrust aside the alien, and do not fear me, says the Lord of hosts.

☐ John 14:18

"I will not leave you orphaned; I am coming to you.

☐ James 1:27

Religion that is pure and undefiled before God, the Father, is this: to care for orphans and widows in their distress, and to keep oneself unstained by the world.

"Candido's Story, continued:

For sure, there were great times that we all enjoyed with Candido, including this memorable Christmas photo when he dressed as St. Nick. We found a technician who made a great prosthetic leg for him, and others who helped his adjustment to the US. But Candido's struggles were enormous and affected our entire family, and his violent moments became more frequent and more intense. He got in more and more trouble at school and a few times the police became involved. Several times, he and I had to appear in juvenile court and family services.

As a last resort, Candido was moved to a residential treatment center, where he lived on and off for several months. There Candido considered suicide, ran away, and presented great difficulties for the staff because of his temper and moods. Their plan came down to this: admit Candido to a 2-year residential treatment center in Vermont where he could obtain the treatment required to settle down and become a functional part of our society.

It was at this time that Candido, his therapist, and I had a long visit. It was my opinion that Candido was not brought to the US to live in a residential center for two years where he might even get worse! This almost seemed like a death sentence for my troubled son. After much prayer and discussion, we decided it would be best for Candido to return to Mozambique. The pain I walked through to come to this difficult decision is indescribable and I felt that I had failed Candido—and that I had heard God's call to adopt this boy incorrectly."

WESLEY AND ORPHANS

John Wesley took these Biblical passages about orphans seriously. As a person of "One Book," he knew that the Bible made frequent references to caring for orphans. He was also convinced that serving those in need were the works of mercy—one of the means of grace through which we grow closer to God and God's gifts of grace and love in our journey towards perfection.

Wesley began his life of service to those in need, including The Orphan, as a young man, as Richard Heitzenrater writes:

> In his early years at Oxford, Wesley demonstrated a concern for the widows, orphans, and prisoners in the city. He contributed to the Grey-Coat Society in town (a charity school). He helped provide a teacher for poor children in a school that William Morgan had started, by which the Methodists taught at least twenty poor children . . . . He gave of his resources to many in Oxford who lacked the necessities of life . . . . In some instances, he bought flax for children in the workhouse to use, and he gave food to families for their health and strength. (Heitzenrater 2002:25–6)

In addition to these personal practices, Wesley had an experience at Oxford that must have shaken him to his core: in his sermon *On Dress,* (Sermon 88, December 30, 1786) he relates an experience he had while he was still at Oxford. His recounting of this story some 50 years later speaks for itself and the impact it had on the young theologian:

> Many years ago, when I was at Oxford, in a cold winter's day, a young maid (one of those we kept at school) called upon me. I said, "You seem half-starved. Have you nothing to cover you but that thin linen gown?" She said, "Sir, this is all I have!" I put my hand in my pocket; but found I had scarce any money left, having just paid away what I had. It immediately struck me, "Will thy Master say, 'Well done, good and faithful steward?' Thou hast adorned thy walls with the money which might have screened this poor creature from the cold! O justice! O mercy! Are not these pictures the blood of this poor maid?" See thy expensive apparel in the same light; thy gown, hat, head-dress! Ev-

erything about thee which cost more than Christian duty required thee to lay out is the blood of the poor! O be wise for the time to come! Be more merciful! More faithful to God and man! More abundantly *adorned* (like men and women professing godliness) *with good works!* (On Dress, 1786 Wesley 1986a:255)

Whether this young woman that Wesley encountered at Oxford was an orphan or not is unclear: Wesley wrote that she was "kept at school." Young children worked at universities—cleaning apartments, doing laundry, helping prepare the meals—in exchange for food and lodging. Orphan or not she was certainly a vulnerable child, poorly dressed for the winter's cold, and Wesley's heart went out to her. He was filled with guilt having just spent money purchasing framed pictures for his walls—an opportunity cost that could have been used for a work of mercy by providing warm clothing for this young woman.

John Wesley's view of orphans and how to support them was shaped further, and significantly, I believe, by his trip to Germany in 1738. The story of John Wesley's disappointing trip to the American Colonies, his botched relationship with Sophia Hopkey, his return to England and subsequent "heart-warming" experience are well known to most Methodists, but his trip to Germany immediately following this Aldersgate experience not so much. To set the stage for the important trip, however, we need to briefly review his journey to America and relationship with the Moravians to understand his German trip.

During their trip to Georgia (John and Charles departed England together on October 4, 1735) a storm developed that broke the ship's main mast. While Wesley and others were fearful for their lives, a group of Moravians calmly sang songs and seemed at peace with their situation and pending fate. The ship did not sink and its crew and passengers killed, obviously, but the Moravians' calm demeanor in the face of death greatly impressed Wesley. During his two years in Georgia Wesley spent as much time as he could with these people, determined to have what they had.

Wesley, seeking to find himself and his theological center, was, to put it simply, unsuccessful in Georgia. His "parish" was enormous—over 200 miles in length and 50 miles in width. The High-Church, Oxford-trained priest and university fellow was poorly prepared for life on the American frontier. Wesley sought initially to convert the Native Americans, but it quickly became clear that he first needed to find himself. He had a complex relationship with Sophia Hopkey that ended abruptly when she *eloped* with William Williamson (I am not sure that term was in use at the time, but the two traveled to South Carolina and were married in Spurysburg, 22 miles north of Savannah: this generated a great amount of local gossip and Wesley's admonitions.) John, distraught and indignant, refused to serve the couple the sacrament of Communion when they returned to his church three months later. After this public rebuff, Mr. Williamson filed charges against the young priest for character defamation. These events, along with the subsequent trial and personal embarrassment provided the impetus for Wesley's return to England in a less-than-triumphant manner. Within his "failure," however, were the seeds for personal growth. These included his ongoing thirst for the inner peace and calm he had witnessed within the Moravians.

John Wesley met Moravian Peter Böhler in February 1738, just after his return from Georgia. Böhler was a recent graduate of the University of Jena and on his way to Carolina as a missionary. For the next three months (leading up to Aldersgate) Wesley "shadowed the young German,"(Luccock 1949:69) attempting to learn as much from him as possible. It was through his friendship with Böhler, along with the various Moravian friendships he made in Georgia, that helped him find peace in his soul and reconcile his heart with his intellect.

Wesley's Aldersgate experience was on the evening of May 24, 1738. In the days that followed, John spoke and preached as a new person although he was still in a state of turmoil and unease. Two weeks later, on June 7, he determined to go to Germany—the heart and home of the Moravians—to learn at the source more about this new assurance he was experiencing. Before leaving for Germany, he first made a trip to Salisbury to see his mother, to Oxford to see his friends and colleagues, and departed from London a week later. He disembarked at Rotterdam on June 14 along with a small group of other Englishmen and Germans and spent the next several months traveling with this same group on foot through the German countryside.

On June 24, the travelers arrived at Jena. The following day he and his small group were admitted into the orphan house. Wesley was greatly impressed, writing in his journal: "that amazing proof that 'all things are still possible to him that believeth.'" (Journal, June 24, 1738, Wesley 1850:Vol. III, 81)Wesley devoted a significant amount of time learning as much about the orphan house as possible, and recorded these words:

> There is now a large yearly revenue for its support, beside what is continually brought in by the printing office, the books sold there, and the apothecary's shop, which is furnished with all sorts of medicine. The building reaches backward from the front in two wings, for, I believe, a hundred and fifty yards. The lodging chamber for the children, their dining room, their chapel, and all the adjourning apartments, are so conveniently contrived, and so exactly clean, as I have never seen any before. Six hundred and fifty children, we were informed, are wholly maintained there; and three thousand, if I mistake not, are taught. Surely, such a thing neither we nor our fathers have known, as this great thing which God has done here! (Journal, June 24, 1738, Wesley 1850:Vol. III, 81)

A week later Wesley and his party arrived at Hernhuth, about 30 miles from Dresden, at the estate and headquarters of Count Zinzendorf, the leader of the Moravians. Again Wesley spent a great amount of time observing the orphan house they had built: he was specifically interested in how it was funded. His journal is again filled with methodical notes on the operations of this orphan house, as well as experiences he had with Moravian clergy and laity. While, to be sure, he found fault with the Moravians, he was also profoundly moved by their attempts to create an authentic Christian community based on the model described in Acts 2: 43 – 47.

In September 1738 Wesley returned to England, this time a changed person from the one who arrived back from Georgia earlier in the year. His friendship with Peter Böhler, his Aldersgate experience and the trip to Germany allowed him to 1) find himself and the personal assurance he longed for, 2) sort out his theology and 3) see a vision of the beloved community he sought within the Church of England. It gave him the foundation from which he would, in time, organize the Methodist Movement's theology, structure and mission.

GEORGE WHITEFIELD'S MINISTRY TO ORPHANS

Wesley was given an immediate opportunity in which to put his observations of the orphan homes in Germany into action. His friend, colleague, mentee and fellow member of the Holiness Club at Oxford, George Whitefield, decided to establish an orphan house in Georgia. Whitefield, 11 years younger than John and 7 years younger than Charles, had stayed back in Oxford to complete his education when the Wesley brothers traveled to Georgia in 1735. Whitefield became the leader of the Oxford Methodists, completed his Bachelor of Arts degree and was ordained a deacon in 1736. The Wesley's invited Whitefield to come to Georgia while they were still in the colony, but Whitefield needed to spent another year in England raising funds for his American trip: Whitefield would not depart for the colonies until May, 1738, just as Wesley was experiencing his Aldersgate Heart Warming moment.

On this initial trip to America George Whitefield stayed only four months, but his heart was touched by the needs of the orphans he encountered in the Georgia colony and it was during this time that he decided to dedicate his life to the service of orphans. He returned to England to raise funds for the establishment of an orphanage near Savannah.

It was the desire to raise funds for orphans in America that the tradition of field preaching was established for Methodist preachers. Traveling throughout England Whitefield, anticipating the same treatment John Wesley would soon receive, was banned from speaking in many churches because of his irregular (i.e. emotional, spirit-filled) preaching style. In response to this ban, Whitefield began preaching outdoors, thus paving the way for Wesley and other Methodists. He had great success in Bristol, preaching to crowds of 3,000 and more while collecting funds for the proposed orphanage. After several weeks in Bristol Whitefield wanted to move on to other areas in which to preach and fundraise. He invited Wesley to Bristol to carry on the work he had begun. Wesley, at the time serving a church in London, was not too happy to be tapped as Whitefield's "successor," but eventually agreed to go. Wesley first watched Whitefield's preaching outdoors before himself agreeing that this was an effective form of evangelism. After Whitefield departed John took this major leap and "submitted to be more vile and proclaimed in the highways the glad tidings of salvation, speaking from a little eminence in a ground adjoining to the city, to about three thousand people." (Journal, April 2, 1739, Wesley 1990:46)

It could be argued that Whitefield's determination to raise funds for the orphanage in Georgia, coupled with his banishment from the Church of England pulpits, was the prime mover in his decision to take up field preaching early in 1739. Whitefield's pioneering decision to move outdoors and preach in the highways spurred John Wesley to follow suit. We can say, then, with some confidence, that

Whitefield's commitment to the orphans in Georgia was one of the most important turning points in Methodist History.

Whitefield returned to America in November 1739. This time he arrived in Philadelphia and resumed his preaching and fundraising activities for the new orphanage now on the American soil. It was during this time that Whitefield struck up a great friendship with Benjamin Franklin, but that interesting relationship is beyond the scope of this book. Whitefield's preaching, in Presbyterian and Church of England Churches, as well as outdoors, made him the leading figure of the American Great Awakening. When he arrived in Savannah in January 1740 he was greeted as a hero. He had with him £2,539 (approximately $400,000 in today's currency) towards construction of the orphan house.

Whitefield received a land grant of 500 acres about 10 miles south of Savannah, and began construction on March 25, 1740. The main house had twenty rooms and was two stories tall. Two smaller buildings were constructed nearby. Whitefield named it the Bethesda Orphanage, Bethesda meaning "House of Mercy." In 1773 a fire destroyed the original home. Plans to rebuild and expand were put on hold during the US Revolutionary War, and after much discussion a new building and name, the Bethesda Home for Boys was established. In 2011, the Bethesda Home for Boys was renamed again, this time to the Bethesda Academy. Although it is no longer an orphanage, the Bethesda Academy sits on the same property George Whitefield developed 275 years ago, and this is considered the oldest extant non-profit in the United States as well as being the longest-serving child caring institution in the country.

Whitefield's vision was for a loving community where orphans would be raised with strict discipline and his theological blend of Calvinism / Methodism / Church of England. He hoped it would develop into "an oasis of religion in a desert of paganism." (Heitzenrater 2002:227) The children grew most of the food for themselves, but the orphanage costs were more than anticipated. Whitefield returned to England to raise additional funds for the orphanage, while Franklin encouraged White-field to re-locate the orphanage to Philadelphia where Franklin could help oversee it's funding. Whitefield declined Franklin's offer, maintaining that the land and funds had been given for the orphanage at that location and not elsewhere. In 1740, Whitefield hired some of the Moravians he knew from Georgia to construct a second orphanage for black orphans in the Lehigh Valley in Pennsylvania. This is now the Whitefield House.

The Bethesda Orphanage continued to struggle financially despite the fundraising Whitefield continued to do both in England and the colonies. The way Whitefield eventually responded, however, marks a low moment in our history.

George Whitefield, unlike John Wesley, but like many other Americans of his day, was a believer in the institution of slavery. He believed that slavery was compatible with Christianity and argued for its legalization in Georgia—slavery had been outlawed in Georgia in 1735. Slavery was re-legalized in Georgia in 1751, partially due to the lobbying efforts of Whitefield. Whitefield then proceeded to purchase slaves to work at Bethesda. He also employed slaves at his personal property, Providence Plantation, to raise funds for the orphanage.

In 1764, Whitefield wanted to convert the orphanage into an academy. Wesley responded sharply, writing:

> Some time ago, since you went hence, I heard a circumstance which gave me a good deal of concern; namely, that the college or academy in Georgia has swallowed up the Orphan house. Shall I give my judgment without being asked? Methinks, friendship requires I should. Are there not then two points which come in view? A point of mercy, and a point of justice? With regard to the former may it not be inquired, can any thing on earth be a greater charity, than to bring up orphans? What is a college or an academy compared to this? Unless you could have such a college as per-

haps is not upon earth. I know the value of learning, and am more in danger of prizing it too much than too little. But still, I cannot place the giving it to five hundred students, on a level with saving the bodies, if not the souls too, of find hundred orphans. But let us pass on from the point of view of mercy to that of justice: you had land given, and collected money, for an Orphan house; are you at liberty to apply this to any other purpose? At least, while there are any orphans in Georgia left? (Letter to the Rev. George Whitefield,1770, Wesley 1850:Vol. III, 684–685)

Wesley's opinion prevailed—at the time—and although the orphanage was eventually converted into a boy's school this was not until recently, when other means to care for orphans in Georgia—adoption and foster care— were in place.

When Whitefield died in 1770 it was John Wesley who delivered his eulogy. Wesley, an ardent abolitionist, did not mention in his remarks Whitefield's racist worldview nor his ownership of slaves, (Sermon 53: On the Death of the Rev. Mr. George Whitefield), and did not include any words about the theological differences the two had about Calvinism, but multiple times Wesley mentioned the work to which Whitefield was committed of providing for orphans, and how it was that in 1738 George first "observed the deplorable condition of many children here [Georgia]; and that God put into his heart the first thought of founding an orphan-house." (Wesley 1985b:333)

METHODIST WORK WITH ORPHANS IN ENGLAND

Meanwhile, as the Methodist Movement / Revival spread in England, Wesley sought to duplicate what he saw in Germany and what Whitefield was accomplishing in Georgia: Wesley began construction of orphan houses in England.

In the spring of 1742, Wesley visited Yorkshire, where several of his colleagues had established Methodist Societies. On May 30, he began his ministry in Newcastle among "the poorest and most contemptible part of the town." (Journal Wesley 1850:Vol. III, p. 253)

> Before the year was out, Wesley laid the first stone for a preaching-house in Newcastle, the largest of four now under his control. Once again, he had launched a venture in faith, starting the building with only £1.60s in his pocket. He solicited contributions, preached charity sermons, accepted gifts (such as £100 from a Quaker who had a dream that Wesley could use the funds), and generally trusted that the money would come in. He was following the method that August Hermann Francke had used with the Orphan-house at Halle. Following Francke and Whitefield, Wesley also called his building in Newcastle the "Orphan-house" and used the facility for a number of uses, including a school and an infirmary, in addition to the preaching-house. (Heitzenrater 2002:138)

Back in London, in December 1746, Wesley opened a medical clinic, offering free medical care to both members and non-members of the Methodist Societies. He established at the Foundry "The Poorhouse:" two small homes were rented near the Foundry wherein Wesley provided warm and clean lodging for "feeble, aged widows." Roughly a dozen persons lived here, including a blind woman and two poor children. (A Plain Account, 1749, Wesley 1989a:277). In addition, he provided an education for the street children whose poverty prevented them from attending school. "He hired two school-masters to teach reading, writing, and casting accounts. Volunteer contributions also covered the costs of this venture . . . . By this time, Wesley had also built a new Kingswood School outside Bristol." (Heitzenrater 2002:167–8) Wesley wanted his societies to educate those who could not afford schooling regardless of whether they were orphans or simply vulnerable children whose parents were mired in deep poverty.

John Wesley had found his calling—preaching, teaching, writing and leading the "church within a church," the Methodist Movement inside the Church of England. He did so primarily through and with an emphasis and solidarity with the poor, believing that "an alliance with wealth and power must ever corrupt the gospel. That is, there is an inherent contradiction between the gospel of love and peace, on the one hand, and the possession of privilege in the world on the other. Thus, an alliance with wealth and power must result in the establishment of a pseudo-Christianity whose interests would lie in the maintenance of the system of wealth and power rather than in the propagation of true, scriptural Christianity." (Jennings 1990:42)

As the Methodist movement found success, Wesley worried about its future. In letters to Freeborn Garretson in 1785 and 1786, Wesley wrote, respectively: "It is a sad observation, they that have most money have usually least grace," and "Most of those in England who have riches love money, even the Methodists: at least those who are called so. The poor are the Christians. I am quite out of conceit with almost all those who have this world's goods." (Wesley 1831:Vol. VII, 184, 185) Wesley sought to place the poor at the center of his movement, but as he neared death he realized that the poor were instead being marginalized and placed at the edges of the institution he had established. The history of Methodism, perhaps, "is not one of triumph but of failure, of failure to carry through the vision of Christ's solidarity with the poor." (Jennings 1990:62)

Towards the end of his life John Wesley wrote his final reflective piece on the movement he had co-founded with his brother, and titled it *Thoughts Upon Methodism*. This is an extremely important essay, and begins with his well-known phrase regarding the ongoing existence of his movement:

I am not afraid that the people called Methodists should ever
cease to exist either in Europe or America. But I am afraid,
lest they should only exist as a dead sect, having the form of
religion without the power. And this undoubtedly will be
the case, unless they hold fast both the doctrine, spirit, and
discipline with which they first set out. (Wesley 1989b:527)

What is it that Wesley feared most? It is not a concern for numerical growth
or success, it is not about losing our evangelical fervor, nor about theological doctrines. Instead, a full reading of this essay shows that Wesley is most
concerned with the worldly success and wealth his people and the church
were experiencing. This concerned Wesley because he believed that as a
people become more prosperous they become less faithful.

Within this essay (Thoughts on Methodism) Wesley begins with
a brief review of the origins of the Methodist Movement, tracing it back
to his years at Oxford and the growth of the societies. He then proceeds
with this warning:

From this short sketch of Methodism, (so called,) any man
of understanding may easily discern, that it is only plain,
scriptural religion, guarded by a few prudential regulations.
The essence of it is holiness of heart and life; the circumstan-
tials all point to this. And as long as they are joined together
in the people called Methodists, no weapon formed against
them shall prosper. But if even the circumstantial parts are
despised, the essential will soon be lost. And if ever the essential parts should evaporate, what remains will be dung
and dross. (Wesley 1989b:529)

What are the essential parts Wesley fears losing? It is the increase of wealth
among its members and our collective failure to place the needs of the poor
at the center of this movement:

I fear, wherever riches have increased, (exceeding few are the
exceptions,) the essence of religion, the mind that was in

> Christ, has decreased in the same proportion. Therefore do
> I not see how it is possible, in the nature of things, for any
> revival of true religion to continue long. For religion must
> necessarily produce both industry and frugality; and these
> cannot but produce riches. But as riches increase, so will
> pride, anger, and love of the world in all its branches. (Wes-
> ley 1989b:529)

He concludes this "farewell" essay / warning with these simple but hard to
follow words:

> Is there no way to prevent this? This continual declension
> of pure religion? We ought not to forbid people to be dili-
> gent and frugal: We must exhort all Christians to gain all
> they can, and to save all they can; that is, in effect, to grow
> rich! What way, then, (I ask again,) can we take, that our
> money may not sin; us to the nethermost hell? There is one
> way, and there is no other under heaven. If those who "gain
> all they can," and "save all they can," will likewise "give all
> they can;" then, the more they gain, the more they will grow
> in grace, and the more treasure they will lay up in heaven.
> (Wesley 1989b:530)

There may be no greater evidence of losing the Wesleyan focus on the poor
than the decision made by William Booth, a Methodist minister in the
mold of John Wesley, who decided to split from the Methodists in 1865.
William Booth founded the Salvation Army, an organization designed
to serve the destitute and hungry by meeting their physical and spiritual
needs. It is ironic that Booth left a denomination founded to serve the poor
in order to establish a new organization with the same goal.

CONCLUSION

Orphans and vulnerable children are the least, the last and the lost. As
children they have no power, resources or bargaining strength. They cannot

form a special interest group nor hire lobbyists to advocate for their needs. UNICEF today defines 210 million children as orphans: 26,000 children die daily according to the World Health Organization.

John and Charles Wesley founded the Methodist Church with an emphasis on reforming the church (their church, the Church of England) so that its theology and practices would take more into account the needs of the very poor. They did this based on their understanding of the scriptures.

Directly and indirectly they worked to support the needs of orphans: from his years at Oxford Wesley was sensitive to the needs of the young and poor. He witnessed successful orphan homes in Germany and replicated them in England. He encouraged and supported George Whitefield's work with orphans in Georgia. John was committed to supporting the needs of orphans and widows as the Bible he knew so well mandates.

John Wesley died worrying that the Methodist Movement he established was falling away from his missional emphasis and vision as his teachings on discipline and diligence were creating successful individuals who, while earning more income, were not saving and giving to the poor as he had modeled. The personal accumulation of wealth, he repeatedly said, was a sure pathway to hell.

The Book of Discipline, our governing document, does not include the word "orphan" one time. *The Book of Resolutions*, the resolutions and policy statements from General Conference, mentions the word "orphan" eight times but only once in direct reference to actual orphan support.

We have strayed far from our heritage and roots. Anyone with even casual knowledge of the Bible knows that it implores its readers to care for the widow and orphans. Why then are we so slow to take up these ministries?

I cannot find an adequate answer to that question other than to suggest that the vast majority of the world's orphans and vulnerable children live in places far from us and far from the circles we visit and news we digest. Out of sight and out of mind, we ignore these little ones at personal and denominational peril.

There is a better way. In the next chapter I will outline a methodology in which our denomination can once again place our mission and focus on Orphans and Vulnerable Children.

CHAPTER IV

···

Peacebuilding Within and Beyond the UMC

All this is from God, who reconciled us to himself through Christ, and has given us the ministry of reconciliation; that is, in Christ God was reconciling the world to himself, not counting their trespasses against them, and entrusting the message of reconciliation to us. So we are ambassadors for Christ, since God is making his appeal through us.
—2 CORINTHIANS 5: 18 – 20

I look on all the world as my parish.
—JOHN WESLEY, JUNE 11 1739

From Mexico south through Central and South America, across the South Atlantic Ocean to sub-Saharan Africa, north through the war-torn Middle East and continuing east through Afghanistan, Pakistan, India, Bangladesh, Myanmar, China and North Korea one can find orphans in every village, township and city. These children's future is tenuous. John Wesley once declared that he saw the whole world as his parish. Today, though, many UMC clergy see their parish as their world. Beset by the demands of weekly preaching, teaching, baptisms, weddings, funerals, youth ministry, home visits, counseling, meetings, financial concerns and prayer we become blind to the needs of our neighbors scattered across the face of the planet.

"I want to show you this. Hassan is an intellectually and developmentally disabled Egyptian boy of 14 who I met while visiting Egypt in 2013. Hassan has been living at this orphanage since age 1 when, according to the administrators at the orphanage, his parents abandoned him on a busy street in Cairo. From the police to social service professionals, he eventually ended up at this orphanage where a mixture of intellectually and developmentally disabled children reside. The more able children are taught both personal living skills and training that allows them to work for pay outside this institution. Some move towards group homes, but few will ever achieve independent living. Hassan is likely to remain in this orphanage his entire life.

This orphanage is relatively clean and while the children seemed healthy and happy, conditions were far from perfect; since the initial protests in Tahir Square and subsequent overthrow of two governments, Egypt's tourism has been greatly reduced. This has created economic problems for the entire nation. Like everything else in Egypt, social services were severely cut. Hassan lives in a small room with seven other boys, and daily activities are primarily centered around the TV, which is on day and night. Understaffed and under-resourced, the caretakers do the best they can given the circumstances.

The needs of intellectually and developmentally disabled OVC are enormous, underscoring another component to be addressed.

I know that it is tempting to retreat from the world's problems in the face of how daunting they present themselves. None of us, by ourselves, can significantly mitigate the daily death toll of these innocent children—and so we do little. None of us, by ourselves, can significantly change the international policies of the US or Russia: we have not a clue on how to stop ISIS from its recruitment programs and reign of terror in Iraq and Syria. We cannot, by ourselves, stop global climate change, reduce the number and scope of the world's stockpile of weapons that range from pistols to nuclear weapons, and we cannot end the suffering of one billion children who live in conditions of extreme poverty, one crisis away from becoming part of the 26,000 daily death statistics. We feel impotent.

But there is one international community / agency / institution in which ordinary Christians have some influence. What is that organization? It is the church! What would happen if millions of United Methodists in the US and Europe teamed with our brothers and sisters in Africa, Asia, Central and South America to stem the tide of human suffering and work for a world of peace and justice? What would happen if millions of United Methodists began taking the words of Jesus and methods of John Wesley seriously?

Further, imagine what would happen if those of us who are members of the Methodist Federation of Social Action saw those in the Good News field not as enemies, but as partners in building a better world? What if those of us who are members of Good News saw those in the MFSA camp not as enemies, but as partners in building a better world? What if those of us in the middle saw neither Good News nor MFSA as enemies but as potential partners, coworkers in service to those in need? What if the UMC, as a denomination, were willing, as an institution, to put aside theological and political differences and work together to solve one of humanity's longest running concerns—the suffering of orphans and vulnerable children? Beyond that, what would happen if other communities of faith, from other Christian denominations to interfaith and international religions, decided to band together with us to solve this crisis? The answer to these questions would be, of course, miraculous.

THE BETTER WAY

Caring for the needs of orphans and vulnerable children can be the balm than not only unifies the United Methodist Church, this ministry can also be the means through which to unite the Abrahamic Religions and foster peace with justice in this age of terrorism and religious conflict. But it will not be an easy task: decades of bitter infighting and theological debate have led to deep divisions and a vicious cycle of anger and resentment. Fortunately, it is never to late to begin the healing process.

PEACEBUILDING WITHIN THE UNITED METHODIST CHURCH

The United Methodist Church is not united: a chasm has opened between those of opposing theological and political perspectives that has dramatically split the denomination. Understood on one level as a split between the Children of Athens and the Children of Jerusalem, this division manifests itself over a variety of topics focused on Biblical interpretation and understanding. On the one hand are those who accept the Word of God as divinely inspired and, generally speaking, literally true: the other hand belongs to those who see the Bible as divinely inspired but shaped through human hands whose message is to be accepted on a more symbolic level. These differences are revealed in theological discussions ranging from whether Adam and Eve, Noah and the Ark and other Biblical stories are historically true people and events to whether you must confess faith in Jesus Christ to enter heaven. The most divisive issue today is the topic of homosexuality where the question is if the sexual practices of those within the LGBTQ community are compatible with Christianity.

A denomination that debates is also likely to be a denomination in decline. If the current trend continues unabated, by the year 2050, members of the UMC will represent approximately one percent of the US population.

There is an alternative.

While it is true that theology and theological discussions / debates are important, we as a denomination should be defined by more than what divides us. Our name implies that we are more than just Methodists: we are **United Methodists**.

Of course, we have not always been United Methodists. Or even united. Throughout our church's history there have been periods during which we were divided and at odds with each other. The most pronounced issue from our denomination's history was the topic of slavery that divided the church north and south.

John Wesley was deeply opposed to slavery and considered it to be a great evil. In 1743 he wrote the General Rules that prohibited "the buying or selling the bodies and souls of men, women and children, with an intention to enslave them." Thirty years later he wrote *Thoughts Upon Slavery* (1774), condemning the enslavement of African men and women by "barbarous and inferior white men." Francis Asbury and Thomas Coke, elected bishops at the founding of our denomination at the Christmas Conference in 1784, shared Wesley's anti-slavery sentiments. In fact, "of all the early leaders [of the Methodist Church in America], George Whitefield was the only one not completely against slavery." (Norwood 1974:186)

But in time the majority of clergy and laity in the southern states moved away from the opinion of Wesley, Coke and Asbury and the camp of George Whitefield. Although the Christmas Conference of 1784 required persons affiliated with the Methodists to sell any slaves within one year (with a few exceptions), there were others who, shaped by the culture in which they lived, believed that the institution of slavery was compatible with Christianity. Bit by bit, compromises were made within the General Rules in which the prohibitions against the practice of slavery were eliminated. Like the nation itself that could not solve the issue of slavery at the constitutional convention of 1787, the issue simmered, growing more intense as each side became more entrenched in their positions. In New England and throughout the northern states, the abolitionists became more and more determined to end, using Wesley's words, "American slavery, the vilest that ever saw the sun," (Heitzenrater 2013:307) within the church and nation. In the southern states the transition to cotton to supplement tobacco and other crops led to the generally accepted belief that without slaves the economy of the region would collapse: it was Thomas Jefferson who wrote that maintaining slavery was like holding "a wolf by the ear, and we can neither hold him, nor safely let him go."

The issue came to a head for the Methodist Episcopal Church in 1844, 17 years before the outbreak of the US Civil War. The catalyst was Bishop James O. Andrew, from Georgia, who married a woman who had inherited slaves from the estate of her late husband. Ownership of the slaves was transferred to Bishop Andrew who, by Georgia law, was prohibited from freeing the slaves. The ownership of slaves by a bishop gave both sides in this debate a rallying point and line in the sand that had to be settled.

General Conference that year lasted for six weeks!!! Finally, after much discussion, debate and prayer, a vote was taken asking for Bishop Andrew's resignation—a vote that led to schism. General Conference ended with the understanding that the denomination was splitting. By May 1845, the Methodist Episcopal Church, South, had been formed. This rift was not healed until 1939, 74 years after the Civil War ended. We Methodists may not know how to resolve a controversy, but we certainly know how to hold a grudge.

Foiled against the great division within our denomination over the issue of slavery was the unity found in the aftermath of WWI that culminated in the Centenary Campaign of 1919.

The Centenary Campaign was a mission-based effort designed to both celebrate the 100th anniversary of the Methodist Missionary Society (established in 1819) and "raise millions of dollars for foreign missions, for home missions, and for relief work in a Europe devastated by war [World War I]." (Shaller 2004:97) Both branches of the Methodist Episcopal Church, North and South, came together to support the campaign, a portent of the merger that would take place 20 years later. During the summer of 1919, more than one million Methodists traveled to Columbus, Ohio to support this campaign. They participated in a mixture revival / camp meeting / world's fair with worship, speakers, dramatic recreations of Methodist history and the organization and training of over 100,000 "minutemen" who were enlisted as volunteers to spearhead this effort in local congregations across the nation. Total pledges from the northern congregations amounted to $113,741,455 while the southern churches pledged another $35,787,338 for a grand total of $149.5 million. (Lankford 1963:35)

The Centennial Campaign was an important step of healing and reconciliation between the Methodist Episcopal Church of the northern and southern states, and helped pave the way for the reuniting of the two denominations in 1939. Mission drove the path to peace: service to those in need providing a common thread.

Unfortunately, the pledges collected for the Centennial Campaign outpaced the funds collected. This resulted, in part, because of a brief, but steep, post-war recession that hit the United States in 1922. Still, a total of $105 million, 70 percent of the pledged commitment, was successfully raised. How much money was $105 million in today's currency? In 1922 the consumer price index stood at 16.3: in early 2015 the price index stood at 233, meaning that $105 million in 1922 would be equivalent to $1.5 billion in 2015. Despite the failure to meet the pledged total, the campaign was successful, exceeding the original goal set at $70,00,000 and setting a possible precedent for contemporary times. Fifty years after the Centenary Campaign Frederick Norwood wrote: "Millions of Christians in modest—and often very modest—financial circumstances made very real sacrifices so that millions of forgotten and burdened human beings throughout the world might receive a measure of material and spiritual succor." (Norwood 1974:401)

This is a time in which we can once again unite around a common theme and be about the mission and ministry of Jesus. **The plight of orphans and vulnerable children IS one of the most pressing ethical issues of OUR day.** This, and not any of the theological topics we debate so well and so endlessly, will be how we are ultimately judged through the fruit of our faith and actions. With multiple paths leading into the future we have a choice to make. Shall we continue doing what we have been doing for the previous half century, or should we turn towards a new direction?

The Centenary Campaign of 1919 offers us a model and template. Today the denomination is in the midst of a $75 million campaign called "Imagine No Malaria." Congregations from across the theological and political spectrum are participating in this simple, direct campaign. The campaign has widespread support, from children and youth in Sunday Schools and youth groups, to young adults, adult ministries and seniors. The campaign, along with "Nothing But Nets" and other efforts from organizations such as the Bill and Melinda Gates Foundation and the United Nations Millennium Development Goals, is working: since 2000 the number of malaria-related deaths in Africa has been cut in half, from one million to 500,000 annually.

To raise the goal of $75 million in a denomination of 7.25 million persons, an average of just over $10 per person must be collected. As of this writing it seems likely we will meet this target. United Methodists still have methodical organizational skills and a passion for those in need. This campaign shows that our denomination still had a pulse and when we find a cause we believe in we are willing to give.

The Orphan and Vulnerable Children present another such opportunity. Thirty times the Bible directs us to care for orphans. It does not matter if you are a child of Athens or a child of Jerusalem—both sides can agree to serve orphans and vulnerable children.

We are fast approaching the bi-centennial of the establishment of the Mission Society of the Methodist Episcopal Church, and the centennial of the Centenary Campaign. This seems like an ideal time for our denomination to come together around a central, timely, desperately needed, Bible-based unified mission. Can there be a better choice than serving the needs of orphans and vulnerable children?

☐ 1819   Establishment of the Mission Society
☐ 1919   Centennial Celebration: Methodists in the North and
           South raise $105 million to help rebuild war-torn Europe
☐ 2019   Bi-Centennial Celebration? Focus on serving OVC?

The United Methodist Church can reclaim its mojo and reverse its half-century of decline by adopting orphans and vulnerable children as its missional priority. We can be known as the denomination that is united around a central purpose: orphans and vulnerable children.

The next logical step for the denomination would be to establish a goal of celebrating the bicentennial of the establishment of the Methodist Mission Society—the bicentennial will be in 2019. From there we can establish a goal of raising a certain amount of money for orphans and vulnerable children, and then disperse those funds through the organizational structure already established through the four areas of focus that can be brought together under the overall banner of orphans and vulnerable children.

To match the results of the Centenary Campaign of 1819 the United Methodist Church would need to raise the sum of $1.5 billion. Based on a membership in the US of 7.25 million this would mean an average donation of just over $2,000 per member. Is such a campaign possible? I believe it is.

"Candido's Story, continued:

Returning with Candido to Mozambique was one of the saddest moments of my life. But as the time to depart neared, Candido's spirit seemed to improve; he was, in my respects, looking forward to returning to his homeland.

Fortunately, by the time Candido and I returned to Mozambique in 2006 the orphans I had met him had been moved to Cambine and were now living in the Carolyn Beleshe Orphanage (CBO) due to the joint efforts of the church I was serving at the time (the New Milford UMC in New Milford, CT) and the Women's Division of the Mozambique UMC. He was reunited with friends and moved into one of the new buildings with running water and electricity, with access to more food, a health care clinic, and interaction with other children.

The new location also afforded Candido the opportunity to enroll in a local school; in 2010 he graduated from the high school as the 4th highest-ranking student out of 400. It seems that his experience in the United States was paying off; during his four years in the US Candido had become fluent in English and was a better speaker than his English teacher. Further, he had learned a great amount of computer skills, and witnessed the culture and lifestyle of a typical American family—great experiences that are hard to quantify. He became a success story and mentor/model for the younger children at the orphanage. His life had turned around!"

PEACEBUILDING AMONG THE ABRAHAMIC TRADITIONS

If, and this is indeed a big if, but if the energy consumed within the UMC through decades of debate can be re-routed to focus on the needs of orphans and vulnerable children—within our denomination—might that not also be true of unproductive conflicts BETWEEN religions. Well, yes. Here is how this might take place . . .

Judaism, Christianity and Islam are in fact sibling religions, and like siblings we go through periods of anger and frustration mixed with periods of love and respect. Currently, the news reports an increasing level of anger and frustration between Jews, Christians and Muslims, centered in the Middle East but spreading from there like ripples across a pond. Multiple incidents and events have led to this current status of increasing distrust and anger, including these recent actions:

- The terrorist attack on September 11, 2001, wherein many US citizens were deeply traumatized by the actions of a few extremists.

- The ensuing US led invasion of two primarily Islamic nations (Afghanistan and Iraq). These bloody wars have left hundreds of thousands dead and millions internally and externally displaced as refugees. Many hold the US responsible for these outcomes, further driving recruitment efforts for extremist organizations. Weak, partisan governments have emerged in these post-conflict societies unable to control their people or establish the rule of law. Local populations are, collectively, experiencing post-traumatic stress disorders, unsure where to place their faith and trust while the cycle of violence and revenge grows virtually unopposed. Many individuals, traumatized by the loss of a family member or friend, seek revenge in their own cycle of violence.

- The Arab Spring of December 2010 has led to revolutionary change of governments in Tunisia, Egypt (twice!), Libya and Yemen, and the ongoing civil war in Syria. From North Africa

through the Middle East, the absence of competent governments has led to an inability to establish the rule of law and
robust civil societies. High unemployment, ongoing conflict, a
significant youth bulge (i.e. high percentage of the population
under the age of 18), food shortages and corruption have created
a sense of disillusionment, resentment, suspicion and anger. The
Arab Spring has evolved into the so-called Arab Winter where an
increase of violence is the common factor.

☐ The rise of ISIS, aka ISIL or the Islamic State in Iraq and Syria.
Its acts of brutality have shocked the world and have led to a
renewed intervention by the US and other allies with a bombing
campaign and an active US military presence in Iraq and Syria.

These scenarios do not bode well for interfaith dialogue and peace with
justice between Christians, Jews and Muslims. Despite the fact that humanity has moved into the 21st century—an age characterized by advances
in technology, information and globalization—the presence of war and
the ongoing threat of future wars remains a stark reality. The existence of
weapons of mass destruction (from nuclear to biological and chemical)
and the seeming willingness of multiple actors to use these weapons places
humanity in a precarious position: Homo sapiens now have the capacity
and means to wipe out life on Planet Earth.

This should be an enormous, existential concern for every politi-
cian, policy maker, academic, journalist and person of faith around the
planet. Humanity may be approaching World War III, an ever more
likely and self-fulfilling "clash of cultures" as anger, rage and resentment
continue to build in both "greed and grievance" between Jews, Christians
and Muslims. Fueled, on all sides, by religiously founded arguments of
redemptive violence and militant worldviews we have the ingredients for
a "Perfect Storm:" war waged by governments and quasi governments,
sanctioned by religious leaders, supported by the populations and fought
with weapons of mass destruction. We are ignoring Einstein's prophet-

ic warning: "I do not know how the Third World War will be fought, but I can tell you what they will use in the Fourth – rocks!" (Calaprice 2005:173)

Alternatives do exist. Among them is the option to stop fighting and start doing what our sacred texts tell us: we can lay down our weapons and take up serving the needs of OVC. Together we can create a better world for these children, work for peace with justice, create binding ties between Christians, Jews and Muslims that, as a consequence, will help dry up the swamps were terrorists are bred by presenting an alternative narrative about people of faith.

Judaism, Christianity and Islam are monotheistic religions whose total membership includes over 50 percent of the world's population. Our religions share much in common, including our common origins in the Middle East, belief in one God, an emphasis in our sacred texts towards social justice and belief in an afterlife (Jews are less committed on this concept than Christians and Muslims). Judaism, Christianity and Islam also have this in common: there are multiple passages in our sacred texts calling on believers to care for orphans.

In Chapter 3, I listed Biblical verses found in the Hebrew Scriptures (Old Testament) and New Testament concerning the mandate to care for orphans, usually with the corresponding command to also care for widows. These verses are extensive and found throughout our Bible. The Qur'an has similar mandates.

The Prophet Mohammad himself was an orphan. His father died almost six months before he was born and his mother died when he was only six. For the next two years his paternal grandfather, Abd al-Muttalib, raised him, he too died. Abu Talib, Mohammad's uncle, then raised him. Islamic historian William Montgomery Watt wrote that Mohammad's upbringing must have been difficult: "Muhammad's guardians saw that he did not starve to death, but it was hard for them to do more for him, especially as the fortunes of the clan of Hashim seem to have been declining at that time." (W. Watt 1974:8)

Born a paternal orphan, double orphaned at age 6, raised by a grandfather and then an uncle under less than ideal conditions, Mohammad knew personally the struggles of orphans. It is not a surprise that the Qur'an, like our Bible, is filled with passages encouraging and insisting that believers take care of orphans, like these:

- And they feed, for the love of Allah, the poor, the orphan, and the captive . . . (The Human, 8)
- Therefore, treat not the orphan with harshness. (The Morning Hours: 9)
- (Be good to) orphans and the very poor. And speak good words to people. (The Heifer: 83)
- . . . They will ask you about the property of orphans. Say, 'Managing it in their best interests is best'. If you mix your property with theirs, they are your brothers... (The Heifer: 220)
- Give orphans their property, and do not substitute bad things for good. Do not assimilate their property into your own. Doing that is a serious crime. (The Women: 2)
- Keep a close check on orphans until they reach a marriageable age, then if you perceive that they have sound judgment hand over their property to them... (The Women: 6)

Likewise, the Sayings of the Prophet (Hadith) are also filled with Orphan-related passages, such as:

- A man once came to the Messenger of Allah, and complained that he feels hardness in his heart. The Messenger of Allah said, what translated means, "Would you like that your heart becomes soft and that you acquire what you need? Be merciful with the orphan, pat his head and feed him from what you eat. This will soften your heart, and enable you to get what you need." [At-Tabaraanee & As-Silsilah as-Saheehah]

☐ "One who cares for widows and the poor is like those who struggle in the way of Allah or those who spend their days fasting and their nights praying." [Agreed upon, also in Adab al-Mufrad of Imaam Al-Bukhari in chapter "The Virtue of Those Who Care for Orphans"]

☐ "I and the caretaker of the orphan will enter Paradise together like this, raising (by way of illustration) his forefinger and middle finger jointly, leaving no space in between." [Saheeh al-Bukhaari]

Conflict between Judaism, Christianity and Islam has been and continues to be intense—with much animosity and bloodshed on all sides. This ongoing anger and thirst for revenge creates a vicious cycle of violence in which great fear is created, fear that then creates prejudice and misconceptions between these religious siblings. The prejudice and misconceptions breed resentment that eventually gives way to more violence. It only takes a tiny percentage of Christians, Jews and Muslims, with a total worldwide membership in excess of 3.5 billion, to feed this cycle with random acts of violence committed, they believe (or maintain), in God's name.

But, there is another path. On this alternative path, cooperation, collaboration and peaceful co-existence replace conflict and war. On this path these sibling religions learn to set aside differences and seek common ground. Like members of the UMC we can choose to put aside our differences and serve together, and likewise we can expand our peacebuilding efforts to include interfaith dialogue and peacebuilding at this significant moment in history.

I was fortunate to have an opportunity to live and serve in an Islamic nation. For an academic year I worked as a visiting professor at the University of Human Development (UHD) in Sulaymaniyah, Iraq. Sulaymaniyah is located in northeastern Iraq near the Iranian border and is within the Kurdish dominated region of Iraq.

Never have I felt more welcomed, safe and protected than at that time in my life. Despite the ongoing conflict between Christians and

Muslims, despite the tension between the United States and Iraq, despite all of the acts of violence taking place throughout the Middle East during my time in Iraq I was safe and secure, shielded from any harm by my Islamic colleagues and students.

Beyond feeling safe, I was also able to establish, with the help of my contacts, an Iraqi chapter of the Foundation 4 Orphans. During my time in Iraq students of UHD and other universities raised tens of thousands of dollars for the needs of Iraqi and Syrian orphans and vulnerable children. We held events for OVC in six cities in northern Iraq, visited Syrian refugee camps to provide food, clothing and money to OVC (along with their parents, teachers and staff) and established a mentor program in which university students were paired with orphans in an older sibling buddy system. These programs managed to have not only a positive impact on the orphans and vulnerable children we served, it also had a wonderful effect on the students themselves who, many for the first time in their lives, actively helped serve others. It also created a safe place where we could discuss theological and political issues without an eruption of anger and conflict.

My personal experience is being replicated in multiple locations around the world. There are hundreds of international non-governmental organizations (INGOs) that are actively working to bring Christians, Muslims and Jews together for peaceful projects and conflict resolution, including one in Virginia Beach where I now live and have been invited to speak several times. The trouble is that these organizations rarely make news, where the prevailing attitude is still "if it bleeds it leads." Never-the-less, the path of peacebuilding within our denomination, as well as across ecumenical and interfaith lines, is one we should be taking: this is the logical, faithful, peaceful and just route that will create a better future for ourselves and those in need.

CONCLUSION

The orphans I highlight throughout this book are among an estimated 200 million orphans currently living around the world (UNICEF Staff 2013). Though their circumstances differ they each share much in common—chief among which is the struggle to survive and enter into a productive adulthood. They have the same needs, from physical (food, potable water, shelter) to emotional (friendship, family, intimacy), to educational and spiritual. They all want to be safe, loved and cared for. They are, after all, children, dependent on others to fully raise them.

The United Methodist Church is not united. The United Methodist Church is in great decline. Making OVC our missional priority can help reverse both of these problems. Now is the time to organize a Bi-Centennial Campaign for the 200th Anniversary of the Methodist Missionary Society. We should set a goal and use all of the organizational power of the denomination to serve the needs of these children, the least, last and lost.

Simultaneously, we should reach out to other Christian organizations, and then expand further to members of our sibling religions—Jews and Muslims—and create interfaith opportunities of service to OVC. Belief in a God who favors war over peace is primitive, and religious traditions that support the purchase and use of guns and weapons over the use of social services that improve the human condition are religions that should be ignored. Creating a world of peace with justice will mean that cooperation will outpace competition, and working with our sibling religions to care for the needs of orphans and vulnerable children will create ties that bind in significant ways.

Religious leaders and faith communities that strive for acts of peace with justice, that feed the hungry, provide potable water to the thirsty, that service the sick and provide safe, dry and warm housing to those in need are aligning themselves with the compassionate God who appears in the sacred texts of these three religions. Caring for orphans and vulnerable children is among the options we can choose and could be the sea change God is looking for and humanity needs to move safely into the future.

CHAPTER V

....

A Better Way

Paul, an apostle of Christ Jesus by the will of God, To the saints who are in Ephesus and are faithful in Christ Jesus: Grace to you and peace from God our Father and the Lord Jesus Christ. Blessed be the God and Father of our Lord Jesus Christ, who has blessed us in Christ with every spiritual blessing in the heavenly places, just as he chose us in Christ before the foundation of the world to be holy and blameless before him in love. He destined us for adoption as his children through Jesus Christ, according to the good pleasure of his will, to the praise of his glorious grace that he freely bestowed on us in the Beloved.
—EPHESIANS 1: 1 – 6

I continue to dream and pray about a revival of holiness in our day that moves forth in mission and creates authentic community in which each person can be unleashed through the empowerment of the Spirit to fulfill God's creational intentions.
—JOHN WESLEY

"I want to show you this. Elias, Adao, and Henreques are three street children "living" in a favela high up on a hillside outside of Rio de Janeiro. They were 9 or 10 years old. I met them during a research trip I took to Brazil in 2008, and spoke to these boys through a translator for more than an hour. None of them believe their parents are alive, and only one has any memory of parents—Adao, who remembers his mother singing to him at night when he was a very young child. Members of the community fed and cared for them until they were 6 or 7 years old, at which point they were told they were on their own. Today they survive by begging, stealing, and scavenging food from restaurants and dumpsters. They live together in a makeshift hovel abandoned by older boys who moved to a better shack a few years before. They took me to their home; several pieces of plywood had been nailed together with a sloping piece of sheet metal secured as a roof. Their living space is approximately 8' x 10'; they had several old blankets and slept on the hard-packed ground. Other poverty-stricken children and adults live nearby; they have formed a small community, and look out and care for each other. My overall impression was that most dogs in the US live better than these boys.

Sadly and ironically, their favela is in the hills behind the iconic statue of Jesus, Christ the Redeemer, that was built on the 2,300-foot peak named Corcovado and overlooks the metropolitan city of Rio. It is as if Jesus, or at least his church, has turned his back on these and other orphans and vulnerable children around the world."

REVIEW

The "Methodist Movement" experienced a period of explosive growth and expansion in Great Britain and North America from approximately 1750 – 1850. This growth was based, in part, on a *clearly defined theological mission*, which was to help persons "flee from the wrath to come." Methodist clergy and laity were united in saving lost souls from the depths of hell. One avoided hell through the two-pronged means of grace: works of piety and works of mercy. This unifying mission swept across the North American continent as the US grew. Between 1776 and 1806, Methodists grew in the US by 2,500 percent – from under 5,000 persons to 130,000. This growth continued through 1850 when Methodists totaled 2.7 million members out of a total US population of 23.2 million – a percentage of 11.6. Over one third of all American church members were Methodists.

The Methodist church continued to grow in numbers from 1850 – 1968, but the percentage of Methodists in this nation actually decreased from 11.6 to 5.5 percent. Today's UMC membership of approximately 7 million members out of a total population of 320 million Americans means that only 2.3 percent of the US population are members of the United Methodist Church. If we were to factor in the members of other Methodists denominations, i.e. CME, AME, etc. we can add another 4 million persons providing a total Methodist percentage of the US population of about 4 percent.

What happened to cause this contraction of a once great denomination? *I believe these numbers reflect the truth that our church has lost its theological and missional focus.* We are a divided church theologically and politically that cannot agree on such issues as Biblical interpretation, homosexuality, whether Jesus Christ offers an exclusive path to God, who should be elected to governmental offices and what domestic and foreign policies should be pursued by the US. Our diversity leads to great debates at Local, Jurisdictional and General Conferences—and it has become greatly divisive. Undoubtedly this toxic environment has contributed to the denomination's decline; I believe, however, that **our future as a denomination lies in what we can accomplish together – and not in what separates us.**

It is unclear if the denomination will ever reach consensus on the theological issues mentioned above. But inertia and impotence stemming from theological uncertainty is not an option if we wish to remain alive and become relevant again. The UMC must find common ground, and the best way to do that is to stop the infighting and respond to the cries of the world's poor. Agreeing to set aside for now the theological issues that divide us and coming together in mission and service to orphans and vulnerable children will provide the denomination an opportunity to see one another as brothers and sisters in Christ rather than adversaries as well as to allow the Spirit to move in miraculous ways. Working together and attending to God's mandate will allow the Church to heal and grow once again.

MISSION PRIORITY

Since the creation of the United Methodist Church in 1968, the General Conference of the UMC has adopted Missional Priorities for each ensuing quadrennium. The Missional Priority *"is a response to a critical need in God's world that calls the United Methodist Church to a massive and sustained effort through primary attention and ordering or reordering of program and budget at every level of the Church . . . This need is evidenced by research or other supporting data, and the required response is beyond the capacity of any single general agency or annual conference. However, the ongoing priority of the United Methodist Church both in program and budget is to proclaim the good news that salvation comes through Jesus Christ."* (Book of Discipline, ¶703.9)

The current Missional Priority, adopted at the 2008 General Conference and renewed at the 2012 Annual Conference, is four-pronged:

1. Engaging in Ministry with the Poor
2. Stamping Out the Killer Diseases of Poverty by Improving Health Globally
3. Creating New Places for New People and Renewing Existing Congregations
4. Developing Principled Christian Leaders for the Church and World

The four areas of focus are well chosen and critically necessary. They address the needs of the Church and, if accomplished, and would strengthen the denomination. The four should also work in tandem to create a virtuous cycle wherein each focus is part of the greater whole.

However, they do not work as a mission priority. There is an inherent weakness in this designation: it has four foci and is not *ONE* unifying missional priority. It is too grand to be taken seriously as an achievable objective, and too diversified to achieve unity. Research I conducted indicated that 83 percent of UM clergy and 97 percent of the lay leaders of United Methodist Churches could not name the current four areas of focus of the Quadrennial Mission Priority.[1] The Rev. Bill Easum, founder of 21st Century Strategies, once told me: "If your people do not know your mission statement, you don't have a mission statement."

In his book *Good To Great* business and organizational leader Jim Collins develops the concept of "the **fox** and the **hedgehog**" based on the ancient fable and article by Isaiah Berlin. This fable illustrated that "the fox knows many things, but the **hedgehog** knows one big thing." (Collins 2001) Collins argues that the companies that are able to grow dramatically and evolve from "good to great" employ a hedgehog-like focus and philosophy around one single issue or idea. Placing too many items on the agenda, Collins maintains, dulls the power of an organization because it dilutes the overall message. Great companies and great organizations have **one unifying concept** or theme to which they pursue with great vigor and discipline. No matter how noble each component of its parts is, a four pronged mission priority, Collins would argue, is an ineffective means through which to concentrate energy and become "great."

---

1   I phoned 20 United Methodist pastors and 20 lay leaders in the five states of Connecticut, Virginia, Missouri, Oregon and Arizona for a total of 100 pastors and lay leaders. Although the great majority could not name the four areas of focus it is also true that approximately 50 percent of the clergy and 30 percent of the laity did mention malaria and / or the Nothing But Nets campaign.

Our denomination once had a unifying concept. That unifying concept can be described as the shared message of our clergy and laity to warn others "to flee from the wrath to come." This theme was a unifying theological message of the Methodist church for approximately two hundred years. Those of us over a certain age may recall sermons in which the preacher used fire and brimstone language to steer listeners towards God and a righteous life. Jonathan Edward's notable sermon, *Sinners in the Hands of An Angry God*, is a great example of how preachers used the threat of hell to motivate their listeners to repent and lead a godly life. Edward's sermon was delivered in 1741—at the height of the Great Awakening in the US Colonies—and is a typical sermon of this revival that he, George Whitefield and John Wesley led.

But somehow this theological touchstone for Methodists began to change sometime around the year 1960. Many progressive clergy began questioning how and why a loving and benevolent God could condemn His / Her children to eternal damnation. Although never accepted officially by our denomination, many clergy and church members became more comfortable with the concept of universal reconciliation where all persons, through God's divine grace and love, are eventually reconciled to God.

The Roman Catholic Church has a different perspective on Hell. They define Hell as "a state of definitive self-exclusion from God and the blessed." In other words, humans chose hell themselves as they move away from God's presence and love. God does not condemn and send us to hell: we make that decision ourselves. Under this definition, could it be said that if our denomination, or any denomination, does not go where God is, it by definition chooses to separate itself from God? A church that refuses to respond to the needs of OVC is a church that refuses to go where God is already present, and a church that is not faithful to God's will is ultimately a church that will fail. By choosing to ignore the pleas of these children we choose distance and separation from God, one definition of hell. In contrast, our going out to meet the needs of these children enables us to meet God, through Jesus, in the mission field.

It is not necessarily a bad thing that we have abandoned our historic, unifying theological concept, this overwhelming concern to "flee from the wrath to come." United Methodist clergy, laity, theologians and the denomination itself are of mixed opinions regarding the existence and role of theological concepts such as Hell, Satan and eternal damnation. We can no longer use this as a unifying mission.

But, we have not replaced this "fleeing from the wrath to come" central appeal with a new unifying mission or vision. Theologically and politically we are all over the map with conservatives and progressives engaged in a seemingly endless debate that mirrors the culture wars we see in the broader society. I believe that caring for the orphan and vulnerable children can fill this void and give our denomination the central message necessary to re-unite our *connexion*.

Today's Mission Priority is four-pronged and visually can be presented like this:

Each of these issues is critically important, well chosen and important for the denomination's success. The trouble is that they stand apart: they lack a unifying concept. The current four areas of focus are broad, somewhat abstract and conceptual—and I believe this contributes to the inability of many United Methodist clergy and laity to identify the current mission priority of the denomination. This leads me to believe the UMC does not currently have a *strong or focused* Missional Priority because our clergy and lay leaders cannot name it, much less claim it.

I am reminded of the work of Rotary International, which accepted the challenge of eliminating polio from the planet and has been working on this for more than 20 years. Rotary is well known for its work of virtually eliminating polio.

What is the United Methodist Church known for? A military chaplain friend of mine once reported being greeted warmly by a senior officer. It was good to have him on base, the officer said, because in his experience, Methodists were "the best General Protestants of all."

That's not exactly damnation by faint praise, but it points to our denominational problem: our definition is fuzzy. We're terrific at being undistinguished. We're not known for what we do better than anyone else, but for things we do not or cannot do, like the ability to gamble or reach a consensus on whether homosexuality is compatible with Christianity. But all that can change, change quickly, and change in a direction that is consonant with any United Methodist's values: the UMC can be known as the denomination that cares for orphans and vulnerable children.

ADOPTION OF ORPHANS AND VULNERABLE CHILDREN

As the Mission Priority of the United Methodist Church, the decision to place orphans and vulnerable children at the center of our theological mission will allow the denomination to mobilize its resources under one unifying concept. *Further, it allows all of the current work, programs and resources dedicated to the four areas of focus to continue under the central concept of service to OVC.*

Visually, adoption of orphans and vulnerable children as the Mission Priority of the UMC could look like this:

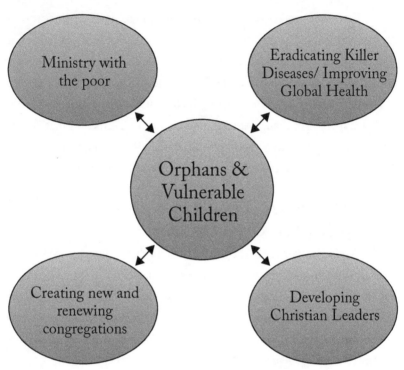

The adoption of OVC as the Mission Priority would give a tangible meaning to these four areas of focus—it will create a visual image that encompasses the four areas of focus in a more concrete and unified frame that will resonate with all ages and church structures, from our Sunday School programs through youth groups, UMW, UMM, general boards and agencies and beyond. Who could be against serving Christ through service to orphans and vulnerable children? Who will forget this is our Mission Priority?

HOW CAN THE ORPHAN ENGAGE THE FOUR AREAS OF FOCUS?

The four areas of focus are, as already noted, important and well chosen. They are also somewhat abstract and fail to form an overall unifying theme for the denomination but do lift up important areas of ministry.

Under the umbrella of OVC each of the four can be given a new status and role as the four pillars supporting the overall missional objective of service to orphans and vulnerable children. Here, then, is a quick synopsis of how the current separate areas of focus can be incorporated under the banner of service to OVC:

Engaging in Ministry with the Poor – Orphans are the world's most vulnerable demographic group with no resources, special interest or lobbying power. They are found in the favelas of Brazil and other South American countries, on the streets of towns and cities throughout Honduras and Central America, in the shantytowns of Kinshasa, Nairobi, Addis Ababa and countless towns and villages across Sub Saharan Africa, the slums of Calcutta, India and other Asian nations – a global total of 210 million children! There are also, of course, OVC in the US: these children range from maternal or paternal or double orphans to vulnerable children being raised in single-parent households and to those living in deep poverty or caught up in the web of addiction or abuse.

Engaging in ministry with OVC *is* engaging in ministry with the poor but gives it a specific focusing on the needs of children: this focus can include pre-natal care for moms, family health and nutrition plans, pre-school programs and improving schools around the world for all ages. When we engage in ministry with the poor we will meet OVC both within the US and overseas.

Stamping Out the Killer Diseases of Poverty by Improving Health Globally – This is the one focus that the UMC has been successful in being presented in a tangible, accessible and actionable form. The "Imagine No Malaria Campaign" has succeeded in taking the broad goal of eradicating killer diseases and improving global health and brought this area of wide concern into a single, focused objective. It is easy to visualize and promote. Our "Imagine No Malaria Campaign" is based on donations of $10 to purchase nets that will reduce the chances of an individual or family catching malaria. This is an idea that is easy to communicate and market to the broader Church. And it is a program that can fall under the unifying umbrella of caring for OVC as they are among the most affected by malaria and other killer diseases. The program can continue with marketing additions to include OVC as those being protected by the mosquito nets.

Creating New Places for New People and Renewing Existing Congregations – The global south is one area where the United Methodist Church is experiencing explosive growth – and it is also where the majority of orphans are found. These children need spiritual guidance and a community of faith. Where there is a need for work with orphans and no church is currently present, a new church start can be created. Additionally, church starts in the developed world can have an immediate mission priority: we can present a unified, denominational concern for orphans, a cause which can help attract and keep seekers who are looking to make a difference in the world.

Adoption of OVC will provide an evangelical opportunity unprecedented in recent UMC history. It will give members of the denomination a reason to share the Good News of what the Spirit is doing in the churches and individual lives—it will foster the need for new congregations domestically and abroad and will put new energy into current churches that are in decline. Going on a "mission trip" will mean the same thing to the Children of Jerusalem and Children of Athens whereas right now the two camps use the same language to describe different events. For Children of Jerusalem, mission trips general mean evangelism and spreading the gospel message in contract to the Children of Athens who see mission trips as efforts to engage in works of mercy by serving the poor. Caring for OVC will present opportunities for both at the same time as missionaries can spread out across the world sharing the gospel in word and deed by service to OVC that will include the planting of churches near these children in need.

Developing Principled Christian Leaders for the Church and World – Developing principled Christian leaders within the UMC means developing individuals who are committed to the Wesleyan Tradition including the two components of the means of grace—the works of piety and works of mercy—both of which can be strengthened via adoption of OVC as our missional priority. Servant leadership was personified in the life and ministry of Jesus Christ, who washed his disciples feet and commanded us to do the same. Service learning is a new component of college campuses where students are either required (for credit) or encouraged to engage in community service: these experiences of working at a local shelter or serving meals at a soup kitchen or providing perishable and non-perishable items through a food bank. Service learning provides the path for solving challenges in the local or global community, deepens appreciation for the challenges others face in life, and develops valuable training opportunities. Students across this nation are developing many talents and skills through service learning opportunities: placing OVC at the center of the UMC missional priority can provide our members with the same experiences and continue the work of developing principled Christian leaders.

WHY ORPHANS AND VULNERABLE CHILDREN?

The plight of OVC is a silent and oft ignored issue of our time. A recent UN report indicated the current number of orphans at 200 million, mostly distributed in Sub-Saharan Africa, South and Central America and Asia. One example of the plight orphans face is within the nation of Malawi: with a total population of 15 million persons, Malawi is home to approximately 2 million double-orphaned children. Without extended families to raise and care for them most of these orphans live and die on the street in little towns and villages or on the streets of large cities and metropolitan areas before their tenth birthday.

In a perfect world, there would be no orphans. Indeed, in a perfect world, parents would oversee their children's physical, emotional, social and educational needs and live long enough to see their children grow up, leave the home, pursue careers and mature into responsible citizens. In a perfect world, parents would watch their children date, fall in love and marry, and maybe come back home to visit bringing grandchildren and great grandchildren. Grandparents participate in family life and rituals, helping to pass on shared knowledge and wisdom to succeeding generations. A natural cycle would take place wherein children would participate in the death and dying of their elderly parents at the end of their parents' long and fruitful lives, and thus becoming the elders of their families themselves.

But, of course, we do not live in a perfect world. Parents and children die at an alarming rate in the developing world, leaving great needs unmet for those they leave behind. Responding to the needs of these vulnerable children in a less-than-perfect world then presents a range of challenges . . . and, with challenges, opportunities.

The adoption of orphans and vulnerable children as the Missional Priority of the UMC will help the denomination find itself—a great need—and rescue millions of church members who are trapped in a spiritual void of self-centered consumerism: have you ever watched the Super Bowl, the Grammys, the Oscars, Jersey Shore, The Kardashians? Need I say more? The US culture is dominated by narcissism and an obsession with consumer consumption. Jesus Christ calls us to the cross and to lives of self-sacrificial giving—this is where little Christs, i.e. Christians, are created.

Working with orphans allows believers to experience the full range of the means of grace by participating in both works of mercy and works of justice.

1. **Acts of mercy**—immediate responses to pressing problems. With 200 million orphans today and 26,000 children dying

daily from the effects of extreme poverty, there is a great need for direct aid—literally handing out food, medicine and other supplies that will allow children to live. This is critical, and screams out to us as the appropriate response. "When did we see you hungry, and give you food?"

2. **Acts of justice**—finding long-term solutions for tomorrow's problems. Systemic issues plague the global south and must be addressed to ensure a peaceful and prosperous future. Funds must be provided to prevent the occurrence of orphans, from a focus on women and their needs beginning at a young age and continuing through the highest education possible, to mitigating the spread of HIV / AIDS and malaria, to the creation of new congregations and development of new leaders.

Here is the key—the current four areas of focus are important, critical components of our denomination's missional priority. The trouble is—they cannot be marketed and understood well, and they do not work well in tandem with each other. None is truly galvanizing as an end in itself, but each can be an important component of a larger emphasis, and should be retained—but re-purposed around the concept of OVC with a central message and missional purpose. Under the banner of OVC, the work currently being done to combat poverty, eliminate malaria and other killer diseases, develop strong leaders and improve the lives of men and women in strong faith communities can continue.

"I speak to my son virtually every week, and we also communicate via email and Facebook. As Candido neared graduation from high school we addressed the issue of what was next in his life. Since the time he had spent in the hospital following the amputation of his leg, Candido has wanted to be a medical doctor. This was his dream while in the US and still his dream back in Mozambique. His success at high school and subsequent high scores on college admission tests made him eligible for medical school. In 2011 he enrolled as a first-year medical student at the Instituto Superior de Tecnologia e Ciencias de Mozambique, and as of this writing is now completing his 4th year of 6 towards becoming a medical doctor. Twice each year I wire money to an account we set up for his tuition and living expenses. In three more years, God willing, Candido will graduate and become a medical doctor in his home country—a blessing and miracle by any standards."

GENERAL BOARD OF GLOBAL MINISTRIES / VOLUNTEERS IN MISSION PROGRAM

A key component of re-focusing the UMC on the needs of orphans and vulnerable children will be the hands-on participation of clergy and lay members from the local church. I have great optimism that there are millions of persons across the denomination who will rise to this challenge and, through works of mercy and piety, save the lives of countless children while simultaneously benefitting themselves.

Local congregations and individuals will need guidance, a step-by-step manual or procedure book that will outline tried and true means in which to effectively serve the needs of orphans and vulnerable children.

Fortunately, we have the expertise and knowledge already—we are simply waiting for the spark to light this fire.

The General Board of Global Ministries has people, programs and mission partners in 136 nations around the world. There is an abundance of best practice, "this worked for us," institutional and personal knowledge among the current and former GBGM missionaries and staff. Getting this information out to local congregations will present some challenges but also offer great opportunities.

I am aware that there is great anger at GBGM by many within our denomination. This anger comes from multiple directions and among different actors within our denomination but, overall, seems to be coming from the more conservative elements of our *connexion*. I have heard many say that GBGM has a liberal agenda they are pushing in their development efforts, and because of this perceived agenda (be it true or not), many refuse to partner with this board.

This division within the UMC needs to be healed. While it is certain that we will never all agree on the role and purpose of GBGM and whether its employees are advocating a certain agenda, I believe the adoption of orphans and vulnerable children by the denomination will allow us all to push the "reset" button and begin anew. Great and fruitful dialogue will take place once we establish orphans and vulnerable children as the missional priority of the denomination—dialogue long overdue and critical for the future.

I have great admiration for the persons who are engaged in the mission work of the General Board of Global Ministries (GBGM). Clearly, there are many committed Christians in the field risking their own lives and working at low salaries in order to improve the human condition for those they serve. The call to mission work continues to be answered by some faithful servants.

My biggest concern in relation to GBGM is the way that mission work—the opportunity to meet Jesus in the mission field face-to-face—

has been denied to millions of UMC members as a professional, full-time class of missionaries have taken their place. Sitting in the pew and writing a check to support a missionary's work in a developing nation does count—in my scoring, as a work of mercy—but denies the donor the full means of grace hands on service can generate. Participation in a VIM team, whether inside or outside the US, can be a life-changing experience and an experience available to many of our members as opposed to the current system where a small group of professionals carries on our missional activities.

GBGM's capabilities have, to a certain extent and as an unintended consequence, allowed the majority of us within the denomination to be removed from the mission field. While it makes sense for the denomination to oversee and coordinate global missional work, the structure and the existence of a professional missionary category effectively denies 7 million members of our denomination the greatest reward of mission work that is *the one-to-one opportunity to meet Christ in the mission field and corresponding gift of personal transformation through sacrificial giving and receiving, i.e. the means of grace via works of mercy.*

Wesley knew it best: the person helped most by mission work is the one who serves. I witnessed the transformational power of serving the least, last and lost first hand. While GBGM projects have helped countless people in the developing world, it has not benefitted individuals and congregations in the United States and other developed nations to the same extent because the person in the pew has been removed from the mission field and limited to writing checks.

There was a day when international travel took place via long ocean voyages, accomplished first by sail that was eventually replaced with coal and then petroleum fueled engines. It took weeks and sometimes months for missionaries to reach their destinations. They stayed for 3 – 5 years, returning to the US to give reports and gather support and supplies. The time commitment needed to be a missionary limited the scope of those who chose this lifestyle.

Modern technology and globalization, however, have shrunk the world and brought the mission field to us so that mission teams can travel to most places on the planet within 24 hours and, after two weeks of intercultural relationship-building, return home to share their experiences. Contact with persons in the developing world is now accessible through cell phones, email and other forms of social media that simply were not possible even twenty years ago: these modern technological advances have generated countless opportunities to strengthening vital and ongoing relationships with persons all around the planet.

Imagine the power of sending, not just the dozens of full-time United Methodist missionaries spread out across the globe under the co-ordination of the General Board of Global Ministries, but hundreds of thousands of UMC members trained and serving as short-term missionaries for 2 – 3 week VIM trips. I maintain that this fundamental shift in who and how missionary work is performed within the UMC will be a paradigm-shifting moment that can both serve those in need and, at the same time, give life and meaning to local congregations.

CONCLUSION

There will be no silver bullet or easy answer in this quest to meet the needs of orphans and vulnerable children and to simultaneously revive the sleeping giant known as the United Methodist Church. We all know that the denomination is currently split over issues ranging from homosexuality to Christology, from Biblical interpretation to the role and efficacy of the church's boards, agencies and commissions. These deep divisions within our community of faith have reduced our ability to be effective in both the mission and evangelism fields.

But there is an answer. Adoption of orphans and vulnerable children as the Missional Priority of the denomination will create a powerful movement in which every disciple of Jesus Christ and follower of John Wesley can come together in service and love. We have learned much, often by trial and error and through great pain and tears, on how to address the needs of orphans and vulnerable children in today's world: it is now time to put this knowledge to use.

We have great models to learn from and partner with. On the secular front individuals like Oprah, Madonna, Brad & Angelina and Bill & Melinda Gates are serving the needs of orphans and vulnerable children and those trapped in the extreme poverty cycle. There are also great models from the faith-based communities as well. Persons of faith will rally to this cause, I believe, and be transformed, I know, as we meet the Christ child in areas of need.

CHAPTER VI

....

Organizing to Defeat the
Spiritual Forces of Evil²

*It is not the physical pain that endangers orphans the
most. It is the mental pain caused by stress from years
and years of being neglected, pushed aside, disregarded,
unloved and made to feel undeserving. Even more is the
lack of unconditional love, the right to be accepted, as a
child and to be loved, as a child, no matter what you do.*
—ROGER DEAN KISER

*It cannot be that the people should grow in grace unless
they give themselves to reading.
A reading people will always be a knowing people.*
—JOHN WESLEY
LETTER TO GEORGE HOLDER, NOVEMBER 8, 1790

---

2   With thanks to Charles Ferguson's whose book, *Organizing to Beat the Devil*,
1971, described how Methodist leaders through the centuries organized for good.

Members of our delegation; I am at the far right.

"I want to show you this. I am standing inside an overcrowded orphanage in Russia in 1992. I was there as a part of a sister city peace project between Norwalk, Connecticut (where I was serving as a UMC pastor) and Kragnorsk, Russia, our host. Given a morning off from our busy schedule of activities, I asked my host to show me one of their orphanages. Clearly uncomfortable with my request, she never-the-less agreed. We spent less than 30 minutes at the orphanage and I took no photos but remain haunted by the experience.

The orphanage was divided into a series of rooms for children of different ages, where children from infants in cribs to teenagers lived. An overwhelming stench of urine and feces dominated the facility and the orphanage was clearly understaffed; we saw only four adults caring for the 40+ children. In the infant room diapers were changed only twice per day and the children left unattended most of the time. The toddlers, too, were virtually unattended; what I saw reminded me of *The Lord of the Flies* because children were pushing, kicking, and biting each other in efforts to control the few toys in the room. The children apparently spent their entire day in this room and rarely got outside. Older children had access to some school materials but spent the time I was with them watching TV."

I am undecided about the existence of an incarnate Satan. The well-known image of a bearded, red-colored figure with a tail and horns carrying a pitchfork seems as unlikely to match reality as Michelangelo's depiction on the Sistine Chapel's ceiling where God is painted as an old man with long hair, gray beard and flowing gown. I think of both God and Satan in nonphysical form.

I do, however, believe in the spiritual forces of evil.

We in the United Methodist Church don't spend much time speaking or thinking about the spiritual forces of evil, but we are reminded of them each time we celebrate a baptism. The very first question from our baptismal liturgy is this: "Do you renounce the spiritual forces of wickedness, reject the evil powers of this world, and repent of your sin?"

I renounce the spiritual forces of wickedness, reject the evil powers of this world, and repent of my sins.

Beyond these words, however, I believe in the existence of the spiritual powers of this world having personally experienced both God's presence and, conversely, spiritual warfare and spiritual attacks. Spiritual attacks occur when I am closest to God and working on plans or proposals that I am convinced will help in some small way usher in an era of peace and justice for all of God's people. Experiencing spiritual warfare and coming under spiritual attacks are extremely painful and unpleasant, but also confirmation that I am on the right path. Let me state the correlation: when I am acting selfishly and doing my own thing I don't experience spiritual attacks.

The spiritual forces of wickedness must be happy with the ongoing theological debates that have divided the United Methodist Church for decades. Think of the time, talents, gifts and service that have been devoted to this division. Now, think of that same passion and energy being refocused into the world to fight the spiritual forces of wickedness, be it slavery, sexual abuse, persecution, oppression, war, corruption, systemic violence, drug trafficking, exploitation or other evil activities. Think of that same energy being refocused to serve the needs of orphans and vulnerable children. Oh how we would be under attack!

Consider the men and women who have left our connexion during the previous decades because of our theological infighting, members who have left from both the left, center and right. I can call to mind dozens of individuals who have departed for other denominations, both clergy and laity, concerned about our obsessive focus on homosexuality and either upset at our current position or concerned that we are about to change our polity. Think of the potential new members who have not joined the United Methodist Church because they see a denomination fighting over this divisive topic.

It is time for a change.

The change I pray for and seek is for our denomination to unite in service to orphans and vulnerable children. This change of focus will demand a rethinking of how we understand the world and the church's place in it. It will demand a broader worldview and cosmopolitan perspective that seeks to overthrow the existential enemies to humanity that foster the conditions leading to the daily deaths of 26,000 children—and can be identified as the eternally contemporary forces of pestilence (infectious disease, plague), war, famine and extreme poverty. Despite the significant and substantial technological achievements humanity has made in the preceding centuries, there are still societies that essentially function as they did prior to the industrial revolution. Despite the wealth and comfortable standard of living that has been achieved and established in some parts of the world, deep and extreme poverty continues to exist, denying billons of human beings the possibility of a long and prosperous life.

The widespread poverty within the United States is deeply troubling at this time in our history: the US is the richest nation in the history of the world, with enough resources for every man, woman and child to have a decent place to live, food to eat, access to education, health care and gainful employment. Unfortunately, this is not the reality. Approximately 40 percent of US citizens live below, at, or just above, the poverty line, and millions of children in America, again the richest nation in the history of the world, go to sleep hungry every night.

But the situation is even worse in the developing world. I have seen deep poverty in the hills and hollers of Appalachia, in our inner cities and rural Midwest and countless other locations. I have served meals at countless soup kitchens and slept in overnight shelters—I have seen the face of poverty in the United States in person and firsthand. But nothing prepared me for my first experience of extreme poverty.

As a visitor to Mozambique in 1998 I witnessed indescribable conditions. The nation's capital, Maputo, had an estimated 100,000 street children among its roughly 1 million citizens. Children lived, and died, on the streets. As we moved inland into less populated areas we experienced more of the same. Resources were scarce—food was inadequate—individuals were thin, weak and sickly. I lost 15 pounds during my 2+week time there eating what my Mozambiquan brothers and sisters described as a "rich, Western diet." Having next to nothing, our hosts worked hard to provide for us. I ate with a mixture of gratitude and guilt. That trip opened my eyes to the challenges billions of persons live with on a daily basis, and changed my life. I vowed at that time to make a difference and have tried to be faithful to that commitment since.

Since that initial life-changing trip to Mozambique in 1998 I have been on a spiritual and educational journey different from my spiritual and educational journey up to that time. I still read many of the same theological and denominational journals and publications as before my trip, still read theological and philosophical books and articles, and continued attending workshops on preaching, worship, church growth and administration. But I have expanded my reading to include such fields as economics and international development. I stretched myself in order to be better prepared to serve those in need and avoid offering "help" that sometimes makes conditions worse through unintended consequences. Far from an expert in these fields, I now have a working knowledge of economics and international development and have created an appendix within this book in which I offer an extended, annotated bibliography of books and information in the field of macroeconomics and international development for those so interested. In the following pages I will offer thoughts on how we can, and should, proceed, as a denomination.

These thoughts are offered in an attempt to get a dialogue started and folks moving into the mission field, an ever changing, demanding arena fraught with challenges and dangers but also filled with enormous opportunities and possibilities for individuals and our denomination.

THE NEXT STEP

No consensus has been reached as to what is the best practice of caring for orphans and vulnerable children in the developing world. Generally speaking, those who work in the field of international development, including many at GBGM, frown upon institutional care, i.e. the placement of OVC in orphanages. Most support programs that allow for these children to be taken in by relatives, adopted by known or unknown individuals or families, or placed in foster care environments as opposed to orphanages. Orphanages evoke the image of *Oliver Twist* for many of us, where conditions are harsh and sometimes lead and actually encourage poor behavior in response to the harsh conditions. Children can also be exploited at orphanages (unfortunately, this can also take place among children adopted or placed in foster care as well).

But in my experience and in conversation with those in the mission fields of Sub-Saharan Africa, Central and South America and throughout Asia, orphanages are often the only viable option and, incidentally, the *best* option for children in some situations. Although adoption, foster care and being taken in by relatives are usually the better options, the reality is that in many circumstances these opportunities are simply not available. These circumstances include conditions of extreme poverty where resources are so severely limited that there are no adults who can adopt or take in children as foster children. Examples where orphanages continue to present the best-case scenario are communities where the AIDS virus has decimated a large percentage of the adult population, conflict and post-conflict settings and areas where, due to drought, environmental degradation or other natural phenomena conditions exist in which people are unable to survive on their own.

In the 1990's the UMC Council of Bishops undertook a long and sustained study of the world's needs and, as a result, produced a significant Episcopal document, *Children and Poverty: An Episcopal Initiative* (More information on this document is provided in the concluding chapter to this book). Following the release of this document the bishops interviewed the bishops and church leaders of Africa and asked them what would be most helpful to them. The overriding answer was this: please help us construct orphanages and schools for our children. This is our greatest need.

And so the bishops established *Hope for the Children of Africa* in which they set and successfully raised a sum of $11 million. These funds were used to construct orphanages and schools in every episcopal area in Africa. The program was successful and ongoing: some of these projects are described later in this chapter.

But the orphanages and schools created served only a tiny fraction of the great need. The Democratic Republic of the Congo, for instance, has a population of over 75 million persons and approximately 7 million orphans. The Democratic Republic of the Congo is the size of Western Europe! The construction of an orphanage and school in this nation was a small drop in an important bucket of need and template for more work now.

I have spoken to several UMC Bishops who were involved in both the *Children and Poverty: An Episcopal Initiative* and *Hope for the Children of Africa*. Neither was designed as a 4-year, limited program. They knew that the construction of orphanages and schools within each of the African Episcopal Areas (there were 11 at the time and 13 now) would only be a start. But the overriding thought was that this would be an important step and that more would follow.

I have also spoken to individuals, clergy and laity, who were involved in this work. Each has said that, looking back, this was among the most meaningful work they have ever been involved in. And, for the most part, these orphanages and schools are still being run successfully: they are both saving lives and training new leaders for the church and their respective nations.

An important study by the Center for Health Policy, Duke Global Health Institute at Duke University suggests that children living in orphanages in certain developing nations fare equal and in some cases better than children being raised within the community at large. The study was done to test the theory that children living in orphanages should be moved as quickly as possible into a residential-family setting and that orphanages are to be used only as a last resort. The researchers found that "health, emotional and cognitive functioning, and physical growth were no worse for institution-living than community-living OAC, [Orphans and Abandoned Children] and generally better than for community-living OAC cared for by persons other than a biological parent." (Abstract, Whetten et al. 2009)

The study compared children aged 6 – 12 who were being raised in orphanages with those being raised in community-based care settings within six sites across five nations, those being Cambodia, Ethiopia, Kenya, Tanzania and India (Hyderabad is a city and Nagaland a state in India). "In total, 83 institutions participated in the study: 9 in Battambang (1 refusal), 12 in Addis Ababa (2 refusals), 13 in Kilimanjaro Region (1 refusal), 14 in Hyderabad (5 refusals), 14 in Dimapur and Kohima Districts of Nagaland (2 refusals), and 21 in Bungoma (no refusals). Reasons for refusals ranged from fear of psychological damage to the children to wanting monetary compensation for project participation." (Whetten et al. 2009) The researches employed a two-stage random sampling methodology and interviewed 1,357 OVC living in institutional care and 1,480 OVC living in community-based settings. Table 1 provides the data used for their research, while Table 2 provides the results of their research:

	Inst. Sample		Comm. Sample	
Site (N, %)	Institutions	Children	Sampling Areas	Children
Cambodia	9 (11%)	157 (12%)	47 (15%)	250 (17%)
Ethiopia	12 (14%)	250 (18%)	51 (16%)	250 (17%)
Hyderabad	14 (17%)	250 (18%)	51 (16%)	250 (17%)
Kenya	21 (25%)	250 (18%)	54 (17%)	250 (17%)
Nagaland	14 (17%)	202 (15%)	58 (19%)	229 (15%)
Tanzania	13 (16%)	248 (18%)	50 (16%)	251 (17%)
Total	83	1,357	311	1,480

CHILD CHARACTERISTICS

Age (Mean, SD)	9.0 (1.8)		8.9 (1.8%)	
Female (%)	42.8		47.1	

PARENTAL STATUS	♂Alive	♂Dead	♂UK*	♂Total	♂Alive	♂Dead	♂UK*	♂Total
♀ Alive (%)	11.2	28.8	3.0	43.0	8.8	52.9	2.8	64.6
♀ Dead (%)	7.4	35.4	4.8	47.6	11.9	17.4	3.4	32.7
♀ Unknown (%)	0.7	2.2	6.5	9.4	0.3	2.0	0.4	2.7
♀ Total (%)	19.2	66.6	14.2	100.0	21.1	72.2	6.7	100.0

♂ is father's status   ♀ is mothers status   *UK is Unknown

	Unweighted			Weighted[1]	
	Institutional children	All community children	Community children w/out bio. parents	Institution vs. community children	Institution vs. no biological parents
Number of children	1,357	1,480	658		
Positive outcomes (higher better)	Mean (SD)	Mean (SD)	Mean (SD)	Mean (SD)	Mean (SD)
Caregiver-rated health	4.00 (0.76)	3.72 (0.83)	13.67 (0.83)	0.342 (0.28, 0.41)	0.367 (0.29, 0.44)
Height for age z score (WHO)	-0.96 (1.46)	-1.03 (1.29)	-1.10 (1.36)	0.011 (-0.08, 0.10)	0.074 (-0.04, 0.19)
BMI for age z score (WHO)	-0.68 (0.97)	-0.73 (1.39)	-0.84 (1.27)	0.072 (-0.01, 0.16)	0.113 (0.02, 0.21)
Cognition (K-ABCII)2	4.76 (1.89)	4.43 (1.71)	4.44 (1.83)	0.379 (0.25, 0.51)	0.429 (0.28, 0.58)
California Verbal Learning Test3	7.77 (2.35)	7.22 (5.66)	7.29 (2.24)	0.590 (0.40, 0.78)	0.599 (0.38, 0.82)
S&B Total Difficulties score (0=worst 40=best)	10.13 (6.07)	10.93 (0.83)	11.05 (5.84)	-0.778 (-1.18, -0.38)	-0.968 (-1.48, -0.46)
Negative outcomes (higher worse)	N (%)	N (%)	N (%)	% (CI)	% (CI)
Diarrhea/fever/cough in last 2 wks	269 (19.9)	603 (41.2)	273 (41.5)	-20.6 (-0.24, -0.18)	-20.4 (-0.24, -0.16)
Child sick on day of interview	79 (5.9)	179 (12.2)	69 (10.4)	-6.1 (-0.08, -0.04)	-4.5 (-0.07, -0.02)

1 Weighted means and standard errors account for sampling weights and the complex survey design and are further adjusted for age and gender (standardized to the site-specific distribution of age and gender among community children.)

2 Mean of three K-ABC-II subtests with responses converted to scaled scores using age-specific norms (range 0-19 with higher being better) distribution of age and gender among community children).

3 CVLT score defined as the mean number of items recalled in three administrations (range 0-15)

This study provides hard data refuting the assumption that children living in orphanages fare worse than those raised in community settings. Overall children in these orphanages were physically healthier, scored better on a range of intellectual and memory tests and had fewer social and emotional issues. "These findings challenge the policy recommendations to use institutions, for all children, only as a last resort and to get children who have to be placed in institutions back out to family-style homes as quickly as possible." (Whetten et al. 2009)

COMMUNITY-BASED ORPHANAGES FOR OVC

Although there may still be a stigma against institutional care for OVC, the Duke Study's findings indicates that orphanages are still an important component of global orphan care and can play a significant role in service to these children. The UMC, by leveraging our global network of contacts and through working with local church leaders, can create and sponsor community-based orphanages where tens of thousands—possibly millions—of children can be saved from certain death. We have the resources: what we need is the desire.

I was invited to speak to a group of 30 young African leaders in 2013 at the United Methodist Building in Washington, DC (headquarters of the General Board of Church and Society). I was asked to speak on my research on worldview, public policy, peace and justice within the US and how these issues help shape our foreign policies. The group was attentive, polite and asked great follow-up questions. At the end of my speaking time, however, I was asked to share my contact information on the white board. In writing this information they learned for the first time that I also serve as the director of the Foundation 4 Orphans, a 501 c 3 non-profit whose mission is to serve the educational, emotional, physical and spiritual needs of orphans and vulnerable children globally.

This news was greeted with more enthusiasm and energy than any other experience I have ever had. There was great applause, mingled with tears and a series of stories about the suffering of orphans in their particular setting. The young leaders then surrounded me and pressed into my hands their business cards and contact information: they begged me to come to their nations to help with the crisis they were facing. Each had a story of overwhelming pain and suffering—and how their conferences were struggling with limited resources to meet the needs of these children. From a place of great despair they felt hopeful: if the UMC in the US could focus its missional efforts on orphans and vulnerable children, they could obtain the resources to change the trajectory of these children's lives.

I share this story to awaken my siblings to the needs of humans around the world, and the presence of United Methodists who can serve as on the ground facilitators and guide us towards effective and efficient projects. Venturing into the mission field will be difficult for some but we will meet great individuals who are already there along with the God of Jesus Christ who calls us to service.

In 2002 I had the opportunity to visit an orphanage in Teles, Mozambique. It was one of the most difficult experiences of my life.

The orphanage had been founded in 1991 by then GBGM missionary Carolyn Beleshe. It was established towards the end of the civil and revolutionary wars that had devastated Mozambique for 25 years. An orphan crisis had erupted as a result of the wars and the church was being presented with children with no place to raise them.

Carolyn knew of some abandoned building near a village named Teles that had once served as a leper's colony. With the support of the bishop and church leaders they took back these buildings from the effects of negligence and abandonment and established an orphanage. But this site was deep in the bush, removed from civilization because the plan had been to keep the lepers far from others. These buildings had no running water or electricity and were located just uphill from a swampy area where malaria-infecting mosquitos bred, and miles away from any schools or health care facilities. Carolyn had chosen this site because she had no other options, and with the hope that in time this would become a developed mission center with a church, schools and health care. Soon after establishing the orphanage, however, Carolyn was forced to return to the US suffering from numerous health issues. Her vision was unfulfilled.

When I first visited the orphanage the 25 children were severely malnourished, sickly and unschooled. Subsequent conversations with the director of the orphanage, the local DS, UMW representative (the Mozambiquan UMW was in charge of this orphanage) and bishop confirmed what we expected: each had been praying for years that funding could be raised to construct a new orphanage facility in a different location where children would have access to electricity, potable water, a church home, educational facilities and health care.

Returning to the US, my congregation made a commitment to raise the funds necessary for this new orphanage. Over the course of the next 3 years our church, with a weekly attendance of approximately 300 at the time, raised $85,000 for this orphanage in addition to our ongoing expenses. Six new buildings were subsequently constructed in Cambine, Mozambique, about 30 miles from Teles but a location within a short walk of schools, a church and a health clinic.

Today the orphanage, named the Carolyn Beleshe Orphanage (CBO), is home to some 60+ thriving children and 10 adults who help raise the boys and girls. The children are healthy, well cared for and happy. CBO is located within 1 km (.6 mile) of a church, nursery school, primary and secondary schools, a health clinic and fields for crops and farm animals. CBO has running water and electricity and, thanks to generous donors, a college scholarship that has allowed 12 children the opportunity to attend college or technical schools. To date, three of the orphans have become pastors, four teachers, two agriculturalists and two others cooks at nearby restaurants. Others are now enrolled in college and pursuing their dreams. It is a dramatic change from the orphanage at Teles. Although we did not know this at the time, the CBO is a community-based orphanage, meaning that the children living at the orphanage are fully integrated into the community in which they live. They interact with other children and members of the community, from the schools to the church and health clinic. Church members and students at the nearby college and seminary actively support the children by such activities as one-on-one tutoring, an informal big brother / big sister mentoring program and a special Vacation Bible Camp each summer. Further, the orphanage has a soccer team that plays games with and against other children in the region, and children from the orphanage are often the guests of families living nearby.

The Carolyn Beleshe Orphanage is successful only because of the relationships we have built with local leaders, from the bishop, superintendent and local pastor to the civic leaders, teachers and local businesses. These children have been given opportunities for success because my church responded to this great need.

There are, I believe, at least 1,000 United Methodist Churches that have enough resources to duplicate this experience immediately. In addition to these churches blessed with resources are thousands of smaller congregations that could, in partnership with other small churches, also fund such a project. The lives of thousands of children could be dramatically changed almost immediately, as would the lives of those funding these orphanages.

The cost to construct an orphanage as I am describing will vary, of course, from nation to nation and location to location but in most cases will cost less than the average price of a home in the US. Advances in construction and green technology can greatly reduce the operating cost of such buildings as well, moving the orphanages towards self-sustainability.

It is easy to see the layout of an orphan community I am envisioning that can be built with local materials by local workers for less than $200,000 in many nations of the global south. Smaller buildings where the children live with an adult can easily be located near each other and close to a central dining area where the children eat meals and can both socialize and do homework: this setup create a community feeling among the residents—and then access from the orphanage itself into the greater neighborhood as well.

Parallel to the story of the Carolyn Beleshe Orphanage are other successful stories by UMCs across the denomination. I am including here several other working models to extend the conversation in consideration of what is possible in caring for OVC.

☐ **Helping Children Worldwide: Transforming the lives of impoverished children.** Helping Children Worldwide grew out of the work of the Rev. Tom Berlin of the Floris United Methodist Church in Herndon, Virginia. While in seminary Tom met John Yamusu, an international student from the Sierra Leone. Years later Rev. Yamusu (now Bishop Yamusu) visited Rev. Berlin and spoke at his church. From that initial meeting a feeding program was established for 40 orphaned street children that eventually led to the Child Rescue Center and Mercy Hospital. Today, twelve UMC congregations from Virginia, Texas and Massachusetts support Helping Children Worldwide. The pastor of one of these supporting congregations, the Rev. Wayne Snead (now serving as the district superintendent of the Elizabeth River District of the Virginia Annual Conference) told me that his work with his congregation (Galilee UMC in Sterling, VA) and the orphanage in Sierra Leone was the most significant ministry work he has ever experienced. It was, he said, a transformational experience for himself and his congregation. Wayne told me that he went to help but discovered that the children and the orphanage helped him find himself and his spirituality again: "I went to help the children but they helped me. They *adopted* me and told me that my presence gave them hope." Rev. Snead has now made five trips to Sierra Leone and some 30 – 40 members of the Galilee UMC have traveled to Sierra Leone, including doctors, nurses, educators and more including his own daughter. Wayne's district is in the midst of an "Imagine No Malaria" campaign that he inherited and is committed to fully funding but he is eager to swing the missional focus of the district towards caring for orphans and vulnerable children when the current emphasis is over.

☐ **Zimbabwe Orphanage Endeavor.** Founded by the Rev. Greg Jenks, ZOE works "as a relief ministry, providing orphans with food, medical care, and educational assistance in Zimbabwe and Zambia." Rev. Jenks has created a new model based on the work and research of a Rwandan teacher named Epiphanie Mujawimana, who wrote of her frustration with Western aid organizations: "I watched as these generous people would come to my country, and give things to my people that my people desperately needed. Then I would watch as my people became so good at receiving that they forgot how to do anything. When a grant was completed, or focus shifted to a new area, my people were left worse off than before because they had learned to be dependent." ZOE is an example of a successful organization that is working outside the traditional orphanage model: it developed an empowerment program designed for reaching orphans and vulnerable children: "The program brought orphans and vulnerable children together in mutually supportive working groups. Social workers worked with these children, teaching them skills and providing them with the resources they needed to begin to care for themselves. The team at the YWCA found that for real change to occur, all of the challenges holding these children in poverty must be addressed simultaneously: food security, disease prevention, housing, income generation, vocational training, child rights, community reintegration, connection to God, and education."

☐ **Sunrise Children's Home of Uhekule Village, Tanzania**: Recently a video and article appeared in United Methodist Communications about Kay Oursler, a now 75-year old grandmother who responded to God's call and has been living in Tanzania, working with as many as 60 orphaned children there. (Oursler 2011) Kay, who joined the Peace Corps at age 65, was sent to Tanzania from where she saw firsthand the great need that had been created by HIV/AIDS. Following her time with the Peace Corps she returned on her own and now spends 2 months a year in her home "village" of Hot Springs, Arkansas and 10 months per year in Tanzania. Her local church, Christ of the Hills UMC, supports her ministry through fundraisers and monthly care packages. Recently the women of the church made uniforms for the boys and girls of the orphanage. Kay laments the lack of funding, saying the need is for twice as many children as they already care for. "I've had to learn to have faith, more faith than I've ever had in my life that God would get me through this. I hear him over there, I don't hear him in America. He gives me strength. He gives me everything I need to do the job, except patience, and I do not have patience. " (Laughs) "People ask me sometimes, 'Do you think you are making a difference Kay?' I'm not sure but I think I am. I hope I am. I've given six years of my life to this village. And unless, if I get sick, I'll have to come home, but for right now, I still have energy, I still have challenges, and I still have lots of work to do."

☐ **The Orphanage Home of the United Methodist Church of Nigeria:** Following the UMC Council of Bishops' Hope for the Children of Africa initiative in 1999 a group of clergy from Nebraska traveled to Nigeria where they put in place plans to establish a mission site and orphanage in Jalingo, Nigeria. The conference established a goal to raise $250,000 for the new orphanage, and they budget approximately $2,000 per year for the needs of the children. The conference has designated Mother's Day as a targeted special offering day to raise funds for the orphanage. (Hillery 2011) Recently the Great Plains Conference published a story that the first set of twins from the orphanage had graduated from secondary school, and that another 33 more are enrolled in secondary school now. The orphanage is home to a total of 158 orphans, of whom 100 are housed at the orphanage, 40 have been placed in foster care and another 18 have been adopted. (Agyo 2014)

The Orphan Home of the UMC of Nigeria is a community-based orphanage set in the midst of the Nigerian UMC offices with schools and health care facilities nearby. It receives funding and support from both the US (the Great Plains UMC) and from Nigerian United Methodists. It both provides the best care possible within the institution, but also works with local persons to encourage adoption and foster care opportunities. It celebrates its children's achievements (the Nigerian Bishop was present at the student's graduation) and offers hope to the church. It is a model that can be successfully replicated in many locations around the planet.

☐ **The Gilead Center for Children and Youth:** located in the suburbs of Manila, The Gilead Center for Children and Youth grew out of an ecumenical organization called the Kapatiran-Kaunlaran Foundation, Inc. Since its birth in 1950, the Foundation has been pioneering programs for communities, especially the indigent children and youth. In May 2001, the Gilead Center for Children and Youth was constructed in Pulilan, Bulacan as a temporary residential facility for street children. It has more or less 13,949 square meters and is surrounded by trees, plants, shrubs, root crops, and vines. The number of children staying at Gilead varies but averages 30 at any time: the children are orphans or abandoned who lived on the streets of Manila. The Gilead Center offers a balm to heal the wounds of these disadvantaged children. They are provided with services and activities like home care, educational assistance, medical and dental services, psycho-social, leadership and spiritual formation. At the center, the children's broken dreams were renewed; their shattered lives were restored and recovered.

The Gilead Center for Children and Youth differs from other models in that it works primarily with older children, offering them temporary housing as various life skills are provided. It is also different in that it reaches out to different churches and different denominations for support: while I know of 3 separate UMCs that have visited this mission center, it is also receives support from other Protestant and Roman Catholic congregations. Its vision is a future where the Gilead Center is replicated so that "there will be no more children begging for alms and food, where there would be no more abused and exploited children, where there would be no more young and innocent victims of violence."

CONCLUSION

The construction of orphanages is not the only means in which the needs of OVC will be met, but it still presents a viable option and means in which children can survive and enter into adulthood ready to meet the demands of the world. This solution should not be overlooked. I have a good friend who works for UNICEF: she believes that the construction and ongoing support for up to 10,000 new orphanages in developing nations—each averaging 100 children—would be the most effective and efficient means in which to meet the needs of one million children. Alternatives to orphanages, such as foster care, adoptions and the model ZOE is pioneering in Zimbabwe can also be pursued that might, if undertaken wisely, save another million lives. From these results a virtuous cycle can be created that will generate more interest and enthusiasm. This ministry can spread to other denominations and across religions and be an important component in the creation of a world of peace with justice.

Every UMC in the US can do something to care for orphans and vulnerable children, whether in the US or overseas. There are likely 1,000 United Methodist Churches that have the human and financial resources to construct an orphanage somewhere in the global south: smaller congregations banding together could construct another 1,000 orphanages. With an average capacity of 100 children this would provide for the needs of 200,000 OVC who otherwise might die. From this start more can be done until we eventually are serving a million children or more through orphanages or community sponsored foster or support care. Like ripples across a pond, the adoption of OVC by the UMC can be the means though which the church reclaims its Wesleyan heritage, fulfills the Biblical mandate and emerges from its death spiral towards resurrection and new life.

CONCLUSION

....

*And now faith, hope, and love abide, these three; and
the greatest of these is love.*
—I CORINTHIANS 13: 13

*Beware you not be swallowed up in books! An ounce of
love is worth a pound of knowledge.*
—JOHN WESLEY
LETTER TO JOSEPH BENSON, 7 NOVEMBER 1768

DEUTERONOMY 21: 1 - 9
Law concerning Murder by Persons Unknown

If, in the land that the Lord your God is giving you to possess, a body is
found lying in open country, and it is not known who struck the person
down, then your elders and your judges shall come out to measure the distances to the towns that are near the body. The elders of the town nearest
the body shall take a heifer that has never been worked, one that has not
pulled in the yoke; the elders of that town shall bring the heifer down to
a wadi with running water, which is neither plowed nor sown, and shall
break the heifer's neck there in the wadi. Then the priests, the sons of Levi,
shall come forward, for the Lord your God has chosen them to minister
to him and to pronounce blessings in the name of the Lord, and by their

decision all cases of dispute and assault shall be settled. All the elders of that town nearest the body shall wash their hands over the heifer whose neck was broken in the wadi, and they shall declare: "Our hands did not shed this blood, nor were we witnesses to it. Absolve, O Lord, your people Israel, whom you redeemed; do not let the guilt of innocent blood remain in the midst of your people Israel." Then they will be absolved of bloodguilt. So you shall purge the guilt of innocent blood from your midst, because you must do what is right in the sight of the Lord.

"Candido's Story, continued:

"In 2009 and again in 2013, we flew Candido to the US for his 6 week Christmas vacation. Pictured here are Candido and myself on a whaling sightseeing trip out of Virginia Beach (if I had know that this picture was being taken I would have put my arm around him). During each trip, he was fitted with new prosthetic legs and reconnected with family and friends. To say that Candido is doing well is an understatement, and while there are still many struggles that my son must deal with, I have come to the conclusion that perhaps I did not hear God's call to adopt Candido wrongly. Like everything else in faith and service, God's path and God's ways do not turn out as we expect. But, with God's help, Candido will be a medical doctor in his nation and culture, serving his people for the next 30 to 50 years; surely this will be pleasing in God's sight and a blessing to the people of Mozambique."

As the executive director of the Foundation 4 Orphans, I have been blessed with the opportunity to preach and speak in United Methodist Churches all across the United States during the past decade. From time to time I use this obscure text from Deuteronomy 21.

The total number of persons to whom I have spoken using this Biblical passage is in the thousands. As part of my message I ask if anyone in the audience is familiar with these nine verses, or have studied them or heard a sermon based on these words before in any church setting. I have yet to have a single person indicate that they have ever looked at this section of Deuteronomy closely. It is clearly little known.

But the text delivers an important message. Lets take a closer look. First, it describes a situation in which a murder has taken place "in open country," i.e. not in an established town or city. The text instructs its readers to have the elders and judges from the nearest towns measure the distances from their town to the body to determine which town the body is closest to. Once that has been determined, the elders from the closest town take a heifer (a young female cow that has yet to have borne a calf) down to a wadi (a small valley, usually with a stream running through it) and there break the heifer's neck. The priests shall come forward and "pronounce blessings in the name of the Lord," and the elders shall then wash their hands over the heifer and declare: "Our hands did not shed this blood, nor were we witnesses to it. Absolve, O Lord, your people Israel, whom you redeemed; do not let the guilt of innocent blood remain in the midst of your people Israel." In this way innocent blood will be purged from that community.

Imagine if we were still to practice this ritual within the United States.

So, a murdered body has been found "in open country." To begin with, there would be no need to measure the distance to the nearest town or city because today the boundaries of towns and cities incorporate every square foot of real estate in this nation. So after finding said body it could readily be determined in which municipality this person's remains were located.

The elders of that town or city would then be obliged to find a heifer and kill it in a small valley in their territory, which would be followed by the prayers of the local clergy: after the prayers are said the local elders (it is not clear who "the elders" would be, but in Biblical times it would be the civic leaders, so perhaps today it would mean the mayor, city council members, superintendent of schools, local business leaders) would then wash their hands over the heifer and recite the words that they did not take part in the killing of this person.

Of course, we don't observe this ancient ceremony anymore. I cannot even imagine when the last time this ritual was observed. It is interesting to see what Biblical rules we follow closely and which we tend to ignore.

Why, I ask congregations and church members when discussing this text, is this text important? Why does it appear in our scriptures? How can we understand and make sense of it today?

I believe the importance of this passage is that God is telling us that every life is sacred, every life is important. Every death is a tragedy, every murder an affront to God and heaven. God wants His / Her people to take responsibility over their territory, their municipal districts, and participate in the accountability of all persons who come into the area in which these leaders are responsible.

What does this say for a global village where 26,000 children die daily from the effects of extreme poverty?

I believe it says that each of us is responsible, that it is our obligation to expand our vision, ministry and territory to care for these least, last and lost—the orphans and vulnerable children who have no one else there for them.

When Robert Schuller described our denomination as a "sleeping giant" he was thinking of our theology, infrastructure, resources, membership and international connections that, if awakened, could change the course of human history. Today we have a golden opportunity, a time to get up and get moving forward again. The time is once again ripe to "reform the nation and, in particular, the Church; to spread scriptural holiness over the land." We can do this by adopting orphans and vulnerable children as our missional focus and priority.

We have in John Wesley's works the theological framework from which to renew our denomination: this framework includes a radical economic worldview and his personal practice in which we "earn all we can, save all we can, give all we can." It also includes an ecumenical perspective in which "Though we cannot think alike, may we not love alike? May we not be of one heart, though we are not of one opinion? Without all doubt, we may. Herein all the children of God may unite, notwithstanding these smaller differences."

We have developed the infrastructure through the years in which to make this happen, including a 196-year history of mission work dating back to the establishment of the Methodist Mission Society in 1819. We have successfully centered the denomination's mission energy with 4-year mission priorities, now centered on the Four Areas of Focus which could, with minimal restructuring, be framed around adoption of OVC. We have a publisher, Abingdon, an on-line distribution network through Cokesbury, and Annual Conference and District offices spread out systematically across the nation. Our church enjoys a national presence in the Methodist Building in Washington, DC adjacent to the Supreme Court and a block away from the US Capital, and in God's Box, the Interchurch Center, in New York City. We have a vital and vibrant Women's Division, and a global missionary system coordinated by the General Board of Global Ministries. We have over 30,000 buildings / structures (churches!) across the nation and total assets well into the billions of dollars.

Further, we have the resources to make this happen. From our origins as a movement centered on the needs of the poor we have evolved into a mainline, middle-class denomination with significant economic and political clout. Today our denominational membership ranges from those in deep poverty to multi-billionaires. We have tremendous human and financial resources.

Today more than ever people want to give to a cause in which their money will make a difference. Saving lives, providing hope for millions of orphans and vulnerable children will create a virtuous cycle that will help Americans re-connect to their faith through both the works of mercy they perform and through meeting Jesus in the least, the last and the lost.

Although declining in membership we still have 7+ million members in the US alone. These 7+ million individuals are looking for the spark to light, re-light or add to the fire in their bellies for mission and service. These 7+ million individuals, scattered in over 30,000 congregations around the nation, could serve as suppliers (See Easterly 2006) for orphaned based services around the world. This campaign can also serve to strengthen our evangelism efforts: we will have a message to share and our denomination will attract others with our singleness of purpose. Most of our churches have the capacity to double their attendance Sunday mornings without any need for expansion, and for those churches already serving to capacity or near capacity there is always the option of adding another worship service. Our total membership could virtually double without any further building expansions—enabling us to deliver a higher percentage of our income to this program.

Finally, we have the international connections to make this happen. There are United Methodist Churches in thousands of cities and villages across the developing nations: these churches, with trustworthy clergy and laity, can become distribution centers in which to send supplies to serve the needs of OVC. Further, the world is fast becoming a smaller place. Social media is changing the way we relate to citizens of foreign nations. Many of us have friends now scattered around the planet: we stay in touch via FaceBook, Skype, Google Hangouts, email and more. Churches in remote village now have websites and an Internet presence. Local churches in the US and in the developing nations will reap incredible benefits from forming sibling relationships—all possible due to the explosive development of technology in the last century.

Adoption of OVC would provide the UMC with an overriding vision, unifying missional priority and *raison d'ê·tre*. Rather than endless debates and in house fighting it would provide us with an overriding plan of action that every UMC member could acknowledge, accept and agree with. It provides the world and its people a route to the Promised Land, and a welcome reprieve from the unwinnable fight we have engaged in for decades—because even as one side "wins" we as a denomination will lose.

I hereby move that the people called Methodist and followers of John Wesley lay aside our theological differences and come together to serve the needs of orphans and vulnerable children. Children of Athens, Children of Jerusalem and everyone in between can agree to this critical mission. Theological differences will seem trivial in comparison to the opportunities to save lives. The relationships we will make serving OVC between disparate groups of people will create ties that bind despite the political and theological differences we have.

UNITED METHODISTS AND ORPHANS

I have been frequently labeled an eternal optimist. It's probably not the worst label and, I suggest, does fit. Despite numerous setbacks and disappointments I still have hope for my denomination and hope for the children of the world. Together we can make a difference. Fortunately, we will not be alone in this effort, nor entering this work blindly. The God of Creation will lead us: indeed, the God of Jesus Christ is already in the midst of orphans and vulnerable children, inviting us to meet there in the mission field. And thanks to those who have already been doing this service work for years and years, some templates and the framework for how to successfully work with this extremely at risk demographic group have already been developed.

In 1996 our Council of Bishops released the fore mentioned document titled *Children and Poverty: An Episcopal Initiative*. The document provided the Biblical and Theological Foundations for two programs: Children and Poverty and Hope for the Children of Africa. These two initiatives were well-received by the denomination but regrettably we moved away from them just as we were beginning to get into systemic issues.

Among other items in the Children and Poverty document we find these words:

❖ The plight of children and the impoverished raises critical theological concerns. The Apostle Paul confronts us with the basic challenge: 'Therefore be imitators of God, as beloved children, and live in love, as Christ loved us' (Ephesians 5:1). The primary issue is the nature and action of the God whom we imitate. The church is called to imitate and be a sign of the presence of the God revealed in the Scriptures and supremely in Jesus Christ.

❖ The nature and purpose of God are revealed to Moses as One who sees, hears, and knows the suffering of the oppressed.

❖ Faithfulness to God requires solidarity with and justice for the most vulnerable, the widows and orphans. Relationships of justice, compassion, and mercy toward the poor are more important than cultic practices and are normative expectations of the people of God.

❖ The Gospels identify the reign of God with children. Mark's Gospel declares: "Then he took a child and put it among them; and taking it in his arms, he said to them, 'Whoever welcomes one such child in my name welcomes me, and whoever welcomes me welcomes not me but the one who sent me'" (Mark 9: 36 – 37).

❖ Jesus strongly rebukes those who would hinder and thwart the divine will for children (Mark 10: 13 – 16). He breaks down the distinction between "our" children and the others (Matthew 10: 37 – 39, Luke 14: 26 – 27). He clearly calls for caring for all children as our children. All children are equally loved by God, and God seeks the fulfillment of the divine image in every child.

❖ Wesley's commitment to children and the impoverished went beyond friendship and proclamation. He sought to provide holistically for their needs. He provided education, opened free health clinics, established a sewing cooperative for women in poverty, provided a lending agency, opposed slavery, visited the imprisoned, and ministered to condemned malefactors. Methodism in the eighteenth century was a movement of the poor, by the poor, and for the poor: and Wesley considered affluence the most serious threat to the continued vitality and faithfulness of the Methodist movement.

❖ The crisis among children and impoverished people is, in reality, a spiritual crisis that affects all persons. (Carder and Council of UMC Bishops 1996:Selected quotes, pp. 3 – 6.)

It is my hope and prayer that the UMC will take up the plight of orphans and vulnerable children with all of its resources, from General Conference through the Council of Bishops, our boards and agencies, conferences, districts, local congregation, pastors and laity. But if the denomination itself does not step up to this challenge I know there are alternatives. One would be for a more grass roots approach by individuals and local congregations stepping forward. This model is, to a limited extent, already taking place.

Some congregations within the UMC are already working to serve the needs of orphans and vulnerable children. They are using a variety of approaches knowing that there is no silver bullet, simple answer nor single methodology for successfully caring for these children. Institutional care, i.e. orphanages, are simply one resource in the orphan-care toolbox, along with extended families, adoption, foster care and giving children the resources to be successful on their own. Each of these paths will need to be developed further in order to have a significant impact on this problem and shine a light toward the future.

There are multiple other United Methodist Churches and church sponsored 501 (c) 3 non-profit organizations that offer support for orphans and vulnerable children globally, many of who are doing effective and good work. Many good people and faithful churches are responding to this great crisis by supporting individual orphans, orphanages, schools and clinics. My heart is greatly warmed and touched by the thousands and thousands of works of mercy that are being done daily across the planet, and the missional opportunities wherein we can serve Jesus through the least of these.

But the UMC, despite the best efforts of the General Board of Global Ministries, has no overall strategy or organization structure in which to coordinate and oversee this important mission work. Nor are there enough local congregations or individuals involved in these vital ministries.

I have personally experienced great inspiration from those within my denomination. I have also personally experienced great disappointment from those within my denomination. I think I am not alone with these emotions.

There have been many decisions that I have seen made by church members, churches, district superintendents, districts, bishops, conferences, jurisdictional conferences, General Conference, denominational boards and agencies that I felt failed to conform to the spirit of Jesus Christ. Although none of us is perfect we can all do better. Self-serving, mean-spirited, power hungry individuals and special interest groups have too often put their desires ahead of the sacrificial tone of the Gospel. One of my superintendent friends told me it is always best to have no expectations from annual conference because in that way one would never be disappointed.

On the other hand, I have been greatly inspired and moved by other decisions made my church members, superintendents, districts, bishops, conferences, jurisdictional conferences, General Conference, denominational boards and agencies. When we, through prayer, Bible study and an active discernment process allow God's spirit to be present, great things can occur.

I believe that God has put on my heart a deep and abiding concern for orphans and vulnerable children. There is not a day that goes by that I don't think of the suffering of 26,000 children who will die that particular day.

I also believe that adoption of orphans and vulnerable children by the UMC will reap multiple benefits, to those children in need, to our denomination and the world. Adoption of OVC as the missional priority of our denomination can have these results:

☐ It can lead to a great reduction in the number of children who die daily from the effects of extreme poverty.

☐ It can serve as a peacebuilding program for the United Methodist Church wherein disparate elements of our denomination come together under a unifying banner.

☐ It can serve as a peacebuilding program for Jews, Christians and Muslims, all of whose sacred texts call us to care for The Orphan.

☐ It can help build a world of peace and justice for all of God's children.

With these thoughts in mind, I have traveled far and wide across the US and world seeking to serve the needs of OVC. I have looked for support and help on this journey, with mixed results.

INSPIRATION

There is a young, single mother in Missouri who, after I spoke at her church, requested that I remain at the church for a few minutes while she quickly drove home and back. When she returned she gave me an old envelope filled with cash. She told me that while I was speaking she heard a voice saying, "Give him your money." This money she had been saving to purchase a new car. When I returned to the home I where I was staying I counted the cash: $2,160. Her pastor told me the next day that she was a faithful though unassuming church member, Sunday School teacher and graduate of the Disciple I class. She heard the call and responded.

There is a widow in Connecticut who, after we had set a goal of $85,000 for the new orphanage in Cambine, Mozambique, wrote us a check for $10,000. She told me that every Christmas she tries to make a major contribution to a cause she believes in. She lives in a tiny, old home in need of great repair, has 3 grown children and six grandchildren and lives off social security and a modest savings account she and her husband accumulated during their lifetimes. Her children will one day receive an inheritance from her that won't be life-changing but still something. Her children are doing just fine, she told me, and she is still teaching them how to be faithful Christians by modeling sacrificial giving.

There is a middle age man in New York City: he is a successful businessman and associate of one of the key lay leaders of the New Milford UMC, where I served as pastor from 1993 – 2005. At a cocktail reception he met with this church member and asked her about her children. She responded: "my biological children, or the orphans I support in Africa?" Intrigued, he asked about the African orphans, whereupon she told him that our church had, to date, raised approximately $60,000 towards the construction of a new orphanage in Mozambique and needed another $20,000 to complete the job. He told her to worry no more, and the next day he had his secretary write a check for $20,000 to complete our fundraising needs. When asked why, he said simply these words: "I too was once an orphan. I did this to support others."

I have met General Board of Global Ministries missionaries in remote villages in Africa, Asia and South America whose commitment to the least, the last and the lost is beyond words. I know dozens of men and women who have served in the Peace Corps with similar stories. Appendix I tells the stories of UMC members I know who have heard the call to service and responded in some form. You will read of Kay and Jerry, who have raised hundreds of thousand of dollars and given hundreds of thousands of dollars from their own accounts to serve OVC, and Bonnie, Deborah and Laura, whose trips to Mozambique changed their lives. You will read of Mary, a successful executive who left her job to become the executive director for an orphanage in Haiti, and Craig, who was on a financially rewarding career ladder but instead chose to leave that to take the position of associate director for the Mozambique Initiative of the Missouri Annual Conference. The call to serve is still being heard among some in our modern world.

DISAPPOINTMENT

I have met with bishops, district superintendents, pastors, seminary professors and general secretaries of General Boards: I have spoken in dozens of local churches and met individually with countless church leaders at the national, jurisdictional, conference and district level. My message of serving orphans has been rejected at the highest and lowest levels of the denomination. I have been greatly disillusioned and discouraged.

Generally speaking, the message I have received from these church leaders is this: "We support what you are doing but we are extremely busy with our own programs and activities, and we have no resources to share with you or for the needs of OVC. We will support you in prayer and with our best wishes and thoughts."

There is a church in Connecticut whose United Methodist Women's unit has an endowment and receives over $1 million every year in interest. The church and UMW affiliate are small: I spoke one Sunday at their church regarding my work in Mozambique with orphans and that bishop's request for funds for more orphanages based on the model we developed at the CBO. The message was, I thought, well received and a special collection raised approximately $300. Later that afternoon I spoke to the UMW leadership about the same topic: they decided not to support this project from their endowment because they wanted to save the funds for a potential "rainy day" at some point in the future.

There is a church in New Jersey with a $1 million endowment whose funds (not limited to interest) must be used for mission. These funds came from a childless couple in the community who were not members of any church but left their estate to the UMC because they had seen through the years some of the mission projects the church had supported. I have spoken at this church several times and have requested funding from their endowment for the same cause, to help construction of a new orphanage in Mozambique as requested. The church leaders denied my request because they want to use the funds to help their own situation. Their membership has both dramatically aged and declined in the last 30 years and they are fearful of the future. They want to install a ramp, handrails and a sound system in their sanctuary, all of which will cost approximately $40,000. They are concerned that, with church membership in decline, were they to give funds to the construction of an orphanage they will not be able to fund their own programs and ministry.

There is a UMC Conference nearby whose foundation currently has over $55,000,000. These funds have accumulated through the years through donations. I have spoken to their board of directors about the need for more orphanages in Mozambique: they have denied my request because their goal is to get the foundation up to $100,000,000. At that time they hope be able to donate approximately $5 million every year moving forward. Until they hit that number they won't use any capital for projects or mission.

LOOKING TOWARDS THE FUTURE

I love history, and the study of history can provide great benefits to the contemporary generation. A value of history is that we can learn from the past how our current conditions were established in order to make proper decision to shape the future.

The UMC has a rich and vibrant history filled with men and women committed to "reform the nation and, in particular, the Church; to spread scriptural holiness over the land." Our history shows how John Wesley set a fire on the altars of the Church England that spread to the Methodist Movement and those un-churched. This powerful reformer had a vision for the Church that included a two-pronged means of grace in order to flee from the wrath to come: Wesley encouraged his followers towards works of mercy and works of piety. He said, "Earn all you can, save all you can, give all you can." He practiced this motto, and hoped his followers would as well. He preached a message of tolerance and acceptance, writing "Let all these things stand by: we will talk of them, if need be, at a more convenient season; my only question at present is this, 'Is thine heart right, as my heart is with thy heart?'"

A danger of having a rich and vibrant history is that we can linger in the glow of the past while forgetting there is an equally pressing need to look towards the future. We have a great history, but we must remember that religion is never any more alive than when it is moving on its most recent vision, never more prophetic then when it is speaking to its own time. A religion that fails to light a fire on its altars and within its members' hearts will surely die.

FINAL THOUGHTS

It seems so simple to me: as a denomination we can continue our sliding membership, we can continue to debate, divide and disappoint our members, or we can unite in Wesleyan service to orphans and vulnerable children. There are approximately 7 million members of the UMC in the US: if every member could be responsible to save the life of just one child, we could reduce child mortality around the world by 70 percent almost immediately. Saving the life of that one child would, in effect, save the whole world in that it would save the world for that child. Mother Teresa said it well: "If you can't feed a hundred people, then feed just one." Taking this a step further: if you can't save a hundred children, save one. Together we are stronger than divided: together, we can save 7 million children, we can save ourselves, and we can save our denomination.

Local churches can, under the organizing umbrella of a coordinating and affirming structure that knows many of the pitfalls of international development, provide hands on experience for their church members with orphans and vulnerable children. In turn, we will be fed emotionally, spiritually, physically and benefit from our works of mercy through the means of grace. Church members who return from mission trips become inspired evangelists, unifying their congregations around a central cause while motivating others to follow their lead.

The denomination can benefit as well. Every day I meet clergy and church members disappointed with the overall direction of their church. Adoption of Orphan and Vulnerable Children by our denomination will:

1. Save the lives of millions of children around the world.
2. Move our denomination from interdenominational quarrelling to a central, unifying mission.
3. Help create a more peaceful world.
4. Fulfill our Wesleyan obligation and Biblical mandate.

Surely these are reasons enough.

APPENDIX I

Testimonials

KAY AND JERRY JONES

Kay's Story

Growing up in Southern Indiana, my mother and father were very active in The Christian Church, but my best friend went to the Methodist Church. So, with Mom and Dad's permission I started going to the Methodist Church, where at age 13, I was baptized and confirmed.

From day 1, I had a nagging in my heart that I was supposed to work with African Americans. I assumed that it was related to civil rights in the U.S. That nagging did not leave me through all of my adult life, until 2005. That year, my church, lead by Pastor Wayne Lavender, was sending a team to Mozambique to dedicate the new orphanage that we had raised the funds to build. They had been on a previous trip in 2002 when they discovered 30 children living in an abandoned leper colony, having been victims of the 16-year civil war.

I joined that team and traveled to the orphanage in August of 2005. This was my first mission trip to a poor, developing nation. I was not prepared for what I encountered. I had never seen starving children, children eating from the dump, and so many children without parents. I spent as much time as I could with the children for the two weeks we were there. And I cried most of that time, asking God, Why!

When I returned home I realized that the nagging in my heart was gone. I knew that caring for orphans and vulnerable children in Mozambique was what God had been preparing me for my entire life. It truly was a life changing experience. As a result it has led me to return

6 times in the past 10 years, and to be a co-founder of Mozambique Orphanage Fund, a fund raising organization dedicated to supporting and uplifting orphans and vulnerable children in Mozambique, Africa. It also led me and my husband Jerry to start KJ Education Fund, which provides scholarships for students from the orphanage to pursue four-year university degrees.

The most rewarding part of my mission, is that now I am known by the 68 children at the orphanage as "Mama Kay", which is better than any title I held or could have held in my career as a real estate broker and relocation consultant. Today, the children at the orphanage in Cambine are well fed, receiving an education, and becoming independent adults. Importantly, they realize that God loves them and that through faith in Jesus Christ all things are possible. I know I am doing what God has called me to do! What a blessing to know your purpose in life.

Jerry's Story

When Kay returned home from the mission trip in 2005, I could see that she was a different person. I learned of her experiences there and how it had released her from that nagging feeling in her heart. But, it wasn't the end; it was just the beginning of a new life, a life in mission with orphans and vulnerable children in Mozambique.

I was happy for her, but I didn't see it involving me. My 41 year career in the Food Industry, and 21 year involvement in Food Banking and fighting food insecurity in the U.S., had lead me to start Our Daily Bread food pantry at our church that same year, 2005. Having retired in 1999, I had spent 5 years doing the things for me that I had not had time to do during my career. But, in 2004, I realized that God expected much more of me, that to them that much is given, much is expected. That is what turned me to focusing on others rather than myself.

Our church did not have another mission trip scheduled to go to the orphanage, and Kay really wanted to go back. She kept after me to go back with her. Finally, in 2008 I did. Like Kay, I was not prepared for what I saw. I had never been to a nation where extreme poverty was so pervasive. I thought I knew what poverty and food insecurity looked like, but I didn't. They are just trying to survive each day, and to find or grow enough food for their families to live another day. The government provides nothing. No Unemployment check, no food stamps, no USDA Emergency Food Assistance Program, no food pantries, no soup kitchens, nothing. But, the people are happy and smiling. They are hard working and spiritual. Their faith in God is beyond belief. They are thankful for everything they do have even though we would consider it as nothing.

When we arrived at the orphanage I was greeted with happy smiling children, even though they had run out of food and had no money to buy more. They had been living off of grass and other natural vegetation.

Obviously the first order of business was to go to the market and buy enough food to last them for one month. The second order of business was to try to find out what it costs to sustain the orphanage, how much money they were receiving, and where it was coming from. To make a long story short, they were receiving about half of what they needed and most of it came through donations from outside of Mozambique. This was the impetus to make contact with others who were supporting the orphanage financially, and one year later to found, along with individuals from several parts of the U.S., Mozambique Orphanage Fund, which today funds about half of the orphanages annual budget. We are looking to start and fund a second orphanage in the north of Mozambique, Cambine being in the south. As Treasurer of both Mozambique Orphanage Fund and KJ Education Fund, I make it my business to know that there is always enough food, and that there is enough money for scholarships for the University students from the orphanage. To date we have graduated 5 orphans, and have 3 more at University this year.

For Kay and me, a mission trip has led to a whole new career, that we now consider our life's work. It is a full time job, but each of the 6 times I have been to the orphanage and seen the happy, smiling faces, I know it is what God has called me to do also. Three visits ago, I was given the same honor that Kay received early on, the honor of being called "Papa Jerry". Better than any title I held or could have held during my 41-year career in the Food Industry.

DEBORAH E. ROSE DEMPSTER

The Face of God

Written with love for the children at
the Teles Orphanage in Mozambique, Africa

With anticipating eyes, you see me turn the corner
and then run with outstretched arms for me -
Your warm hug "hello" fills with me with joy,
and I shake your sand-coated hand.
Your dark, brown eyes follow me as I move about,
for you are eager to receive a gift -
a shirt, stuffed animal, puzzle or hat,
something to call your own.
Your small, shoeless feet make prints in the sand beside mine
and your curious eyes look up to me with a longing
as we walk to the garden near the riverbed;
Joy fills me through, for we are side by side.
Then, when your hungry hand reaches for me
and tears stream down your face, my heart weeps.

I have seen the face of God.

Deborah E. Rose Dempster

December 2002

Miracles unfold when God whispers in your ear....and you listen.
"Adopt this child."
Those are the words I heard God whisper in my ear so loud I
thought it was my own voice.

It was 2002, and I was sitting on a concrete slab outside a cold, lifeless dorm building at the Teles Orphanage, in Mozambique, holding the hand of an 11-year-old boy when I heard three words: "Adopt this child."

It wasn't feasible for me to physically adopt the young boy at the time – I was without the means to provide for him – but I knew I could offer supportive services to the child who won my heart the moment we set eyes on each other. I could write, send funds and love him from across the sea.

My experience is not unique. Thousands of other missionaries who have visited orphanages around the world have had similar experiences.

Deborah Rose Dempster, a VIM from the New Milford United Methodist Church, greets several children of the Carolyn Belshe Orphanage in 2005, including Paito, right, a boy she first connected with at the Teles Orphanage in 2002.

Photo by Annette Griffith

In fact, on that June afternoon in 2002, each of my fellow missionaries connected with the children at the orphanage in a profound way, forging bonds they will never forget.

Emotionally drained and silent in our thoughts, as we left the orphanage that day, with the barefoot children in ragged clothes waving hungrily and chasing us in our vehicle, we cried.

Our tears of heartbreak soon turned to tears of hope. When we mustered up the energy to speak of what we had witnessed in the hours after our visit, we realized God was calling us to a mission: to build the children a new home closer to civilization, educational opportunities and medical care, and most importantly, opportunity for a future.

It was by no means a small task. It would take discussions with leaders in the Methodist Church in Mozambique and fundraising back home in Connecticut.

But it was a task we were ready to take on, and we did.

In 2005, I was once again a Volunteer in Mission and helped to lead a team to a Methodist mission site in Cambine, Mozambique, to dedicate the new orphanage, the Carolyn Belshe Orphanage, our church raised funds to build.

My heart beamed when I saw the faces of the beautiful children, including my "adopted" son, I had met three years earlier. They were growing, smiling and full of a light that illuminated the community in a way electricity could not.

Spending time with the children during that visit filled my heart in an inexplicable way.

I have a special memory of taking an afternoon walk with one young boy. We walked hand in hand along the dirt road of the community, looked up and admired the trees, listened to the birds and the giggles of nearby children playing, and understood our silence.

Even though we did not speak the same language, we shared something more powerful – time together on a walk that sparked a connection of the human spirit that surpassed any language.

Tears flooded my entire being the day we departed Cambine to come home. I didn't know when I'd see the children again. But I was certain the kids had a brighter future, now that they had a new home and were surrounded by resources that would help them thrive, and people who recognized them as deserving individuals, and who embraced them with open arms and love.

It's been 10 years since I last visited Mozambique. I think of – and pray for – the children every day.

Over the years, new orphans have joined the family there, and the children I met have grown into young men and women. Many of the kids have succeeded in school and are pursuing advanced opportunities, thanks to scholarship funds. The orphanage grows much of its own food and bakes its own bread. I've kept in touch with my now-grown "son" and treasure the letters he has written, each time asking when I will return.

But there have been sad times, too. My heart broke in 2006 when I heard of the death of one young boy, the boy with whom I had shared that walk. The innocent child had been infected with HIV.

While his death served as a stark reminder of how poverty and lack of access to health education, facilities and medicine as we know it permeates Mozambique and other developing nations, a bright beam of light and hope shone down upon the orphanage at the time.

His death spawned an outpouring of love and support from the community in which the orphanage is located. A missionary friend who resides in the community wrote of the funeral and memorial service: "He was buried in Cambine, in the church cemetery. More than a hundred people attended the ceremony....He was really honored."

But more importantly, he wrote of how the orphanage's construction and presence at the mission site had touched the lives of the children and the residents of the community: "the orphanage is no more an orphanage but a home where the children can get comfort...They are in the family."

The orphaned children I first met in 2002 may have, for whatever reason – albeit war, disease or other health complication, or abandonment – lost members of their birth family, but they have been blessed to be welcomed into another family.

They have been, and forever will be – as I hope all orphans around the world will eventually be – embraced by all those who have open hearts and are willing to share their love, and offer hope.

New Hope

Written after visiting the children at their temporary home in Cambine
before moving into their new dorms, in August 2005.

we are held together
beneath a blanket of blue-black
all of us
guided by sprinkled starlight
walk with curious wonder
toward the angelic sound -
a new heart beats -
together we fall to our knees
upon the sight of this new hope
twinkling like starlight
in the eyes of a child

Deborah E. Rose Dempster

2005

MARY KWANIEWSKI
Executive Director, Maison Fortuné Orphanage Foundation, Haiti

When one thinks of the word "children" usually visions of smiles, playgrounds and laughter are conjured up. When one thinks of the word "orphan" these same images are far from thought and instead replaced by others that include poor, hungry, and uneducated. However what real life shows us is that orphans are children first, and at Maison Fortune in Hinche, Haiti we are working hard to make sure people everywhere learn that.

My work with orphans while limited in scope to Haiti reminds me to see them as children first. It is a constant challenge to capitalize on the efficiencies of institutional living – bulk meals, group latrines and showers, bunk beds ... while also recognizing individualism. It is in caring for them that we begin to realize they must have more input into their own care. My work with orphans has lead me to this point – how do we find the balance between efficiencies and individualism – how do we include them in the process and in finding the necessary balance. If I've learned anything from work it's that most great ideas will come from within! Its harnessing that hope and putting it to work within a system that drives me to work harder every day.

In my "mind" its hard to understand how my choices have changed me. As an Ivy League Graduate with a promising career in broadcast journalism - I can't remember when success for me became defined by sitting on a porch sharing a mango with a child. I just know it did change, I also know that when opportunities were presented to me I had the strength and faith to not let them slip by. In essence I've been able to find a peace in loving. Perhaps when they told you that "love makes the world go round..." they actually weren't that far off. Its been a journey of love. Loving my family, my family loving me enough to let me go, loving my husband, loving him so much to follow him where he needed to be, and lastly loving myself and in that feeling finding the pull to share that love with others not just sometimes but always and constantly.

It is through these loving eyes that one sees the orphan first as a child. Their smile full of hope, playtime full of opportunity, and laughter full of grace.

CRAIG STEVENSON

Growing up, my parents both told me to figure out what my heart was leading me toward. Then, pursue it. During my second trip to Mozambique, Brittney, my wife, and I toured the Cambine Mission Station in Mozambique. That short, two-hour visit at the Carolyn Belshe Orphanage helped change the trajectory of my life in many ways. Seeds were planted; emotion was stirred in me in a way I hadn't experienced before.

While learning about the history of the orphanage, Maria Lina, a nearly 4-year old child at the orphanage, held tightly onto my wife. I felt all softs of the emotions: anger, frustration, sadness, lucky, happiness to be with this child, love, hope and hopelessness together. Knowing the orphanage director had found out she was HIV negative was something to praise God over. Maria Lina forever changed our lives.

After coming home in 2012, we promised each other to never forget her and the other children at the orphanage. We met other passionate supporters of orphans in Mozambique and became actively involved in the Mozambique Orphanage Fund to support those children. Our work was to share the love of Christ with these orphans and have dreams of helping the hundreds of thousands of children in need in Mozambique alone.

When we realized the reality of adoption from Mozambique would have been a long, unlikely event, we felt a nudge to take a leap of faith. For me, it was during a Walk to Emmaus event. For Brittney, it was writing it on a prayer card at church that Sunday I was on my Walk. We both felt God was going to call us in a new direction. Since that time, we have been foster parents to seven children, from age 2 to 16.

Supporting and uplifting orphan and vulnerable children exist all around the world. There are children in need right down the street from my house or more than 9,000 miles away. My continual prayer is for God to use my family to be Christ's light in others, in particular to these children in need. Being present for these children in need in the middle-upper-middle class American culture is awkward and difficult. That said, whether seeing Maria Lina (almost 8 years old) be an older sister at the orphanage to younger children or observing my foster son pray on his own at the kneeling rail at church, I realize I'm working to fulfill God's call in my life – to be an advocate of hope for these precious children.

BONNIE SHEPHERD

When I first visited Mozambique in 1999, it was one of the poorest nations in the world so needless-to-say, it was a very difficult, heart-wrenching trip. Upon arrival in Maputo, we first saw the "street" children who were not only starving for food but were also starving for love, attention, housing and education. That was only the beginning of a trip that would be life transforming.

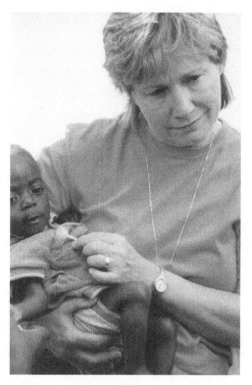

After traveling up the coast to Cambine, our group heard about an orphanage in Teles, formerly a leper colony which meant the children were isolated from society. We were all very anxious to visit. What we saw when we arrived will forever be etched in our hearts. The conditions were beyond awful! The younger children just sat on mats with an empty look I will never forget. We held sick babies and didn't want to ever let them go.

Some we knew were not long for this world. Because there was a shortage of milk, if a baby received a bottle yesterday, they would not get a bottle today. It was devastating. One boy, missing a leg, stole my heart at first sight. Filled with emotion, I vowed that day that I would not rest until we moved those children from that horrible place into a new orphanage where they would have access to schools, health care and outside friends. It was at that moment when I discovered my true mission. My passion for the orphan unfolded! We all felt compelled to revisit the orphanage again and again, which became the focus of our trip.

The plane ride home was solemn and pensive. It was so different from the flight there. The children's little faces filled my mind, consumed me and I knew my life would forever be changed.

The next few months were very emotional. Although we wanted to spread the word and raise awareness of the needs for orphans, it was difficult to literally speak through the flooding of tears. As a parent and "foster" parent in the US, I have always been concerned about the well-being of children, however, seeing these children without a home or family, moved me in a way that I can't begin to explain.

Each night as I lay my head on my pillow, I am so mindful of those children who have no pillow . . . who have no home! And the reality that 26,000 children will die today for the lack of food, water and medicine makes me so terribly sad and at the same time extremely angry! I ask myself, what can we do to save these children and I am constantly reminded of Wayne's question: "Who will care for the orphan"? The answer has got to be "all of us".

LAURA PURCELL

These are my diary entries, written during our Volunteer in Mission [VIM] Trip to Mozambique in 2002

Saturday, June 15th

Yesterday, we all traveled in a chappa (the back of a pickup truck) to the Teles Orphanage. First, we stopped at the market place to purchase plates so all the people at the orphanage could eat together at the same time without having to share plates. The market place was wild! It was like something out of Raiders of the Lost Ark . . . packed with all sorts of things, colors and smells and sounds of people calling out "friend, friend."

Then we were back in the chappa. The ride was a little scary. People drive so fast and the roads are very narrow and full of people walking. This reminded me of Western Samoa in many ways but Samoa is so much more gentle. There is a hard reality to life here that shatters the beauty.

We went down the road and made the turn off for Teles. The roads turned to dirt and then to sand. We were in a "maze" of roads, totally disorienting: we drove on and ended up getting stuck in the sand in the middle of nowhere. There were several huts scattered around and some women and children ventured out to see the strange people who got stuck. After a process of finding and placing palm fronds under the tires and pushing we were able to continue towards Teles.

It was unbelievable to me that anyone could exist in the middle of nowhere but we had arrived and about 25 children greeted us. 6 or 7 were babies and the rest ranged between 4 and 14. They immediately gathered around us and we gave gifts and took pictures. It all felt unreal to me, as if I were in a scene from National Graphic. The children were shy, not smiling, some seemed sick. They were all so precious, especially the babies. We later had the babies tied to our backs and we all had lunch. We were each responsible for feeding a baby. I fed Pedro, a one-year old twin who was not much bigger than my daughter Colleen when she was first born. He ate a huge plate of rice and fish sauce. The orphanage worker gave me milk in a sippy cup but it was so hot he could not drink it. It cooled and then he couldn't drink it because he really needed to drink from a bottle. They only had 2 sippy cups and one bottle for 6 babies! They didn't have enough milk for the rest of the kids to drink so they told us that they alternate days. Some get milk one day and the others get milk the next day. This is so f------ unbelievable and unacceptable! Something has to be done. We were all feeling sad and crying off and on the whole time we were visiting. Leaving them was the hardest part but then again, part of me never wanted to go back because it was so painful! I can't stop crying!

Saturday June 22nd

So we got ready for our final trip to Teles. When we arrived, the babies were all sitting on a mat in the hot sun drinking milk from the sippy cups and eating bread dipped in sugar. I guess that was lunch today. Unbelievable! Pedro's chest was totally congested but he was better able to drink from the sippy cup this time.

After a full day (visiting with the kids, talking with Dieudonne about the farm and malaria due to the location near the swamp, and speaking to the director who said she would love to move the orphanage to a better location) it was time to say goodbye. When I said goodbye to Pedro, our souls connected. His gaze was so intense and deep. We held each other's gaze for a long time. I pray he lives and grows up to be healthy but really wonder at his chances. Lots of tears later, we left Teles with the determination and fire in our souls to be sure we would build a new orphanage and a better place for all of the children we had just met.

APPENDIX II

....

Intellectual Fodder for the Journey

John Wesley was a voracious reader, prolific writer and editor. A "don," aka "fellow" at Oxford University, John Wesley was a strong advocate for higher education. In fact, our denomination was born on a university campus! Wesley wrote these words to his friend George Holder: "It cannot be that the people should grow in grace unless they give themselves to reading. A reading people will always be a knowing people." (Letter to George Holder, 11/8/1790 Wesley 1790) United Methodist clergy are, by and large, well-educated individuals usually possessing both undergraduate and graduate degrees. Many UMC clergy have doctorates in ministry or philosophy. United Methodist laity are, by and large, also well-educated individuals. United Methodist Men and United Methodist Women circulate reading lists and often have guest speakers who engage their organizations on intellectual topics. Many United Methodist Churches sponsor book clubs, adult education classes and other opportunities for study. We are a denomination that honors and encourages education.

But most UMC clergy have advanced training in theology, or worship, Bible, ethics, church history or religion. Most adult education at

UM churches is focused on Bible Study, theology, spirituality, ethics, etc. While, generally speaking, the laity within the UMC have a broader educational base than the clergy, moving into the world of economics and international development with a specific concern for orphans and vulnerable children will require additional resources. With that in mind, I offer this reading list with comments as a starting point to focus our attention on how to best serve the needs of this population.

International development begins and ends with economics, economic analysis and economic development (economics, known as the dismal science). Mixed in between this economic framework are the academic fields of conflict analysis and resolution, cultural studies, geography, international relations, history, political science and public policy. If we want to be more effective in serving the needs of orphans and vulnerable children we will each need to broaden our interests and spread our intellectual nets over a larger sea, becoming at least familiar with different concepts and different authors than those whose books usually appear in clergy and church libraries.

Most United Methodists' knowledge of economics ended with the supply and demand curves we studied in college. As I have struggled to understand and remedy the situation of orphans and vulnerable children over the last decade, I have pushed deeper into the field of economics, from macroeconomics and microeconomics to economic history and development theory. I have read Adam's Smith's *An Inquiry into the Nature and Causes of the Wealth of Nations* and Karl Marx's *Capital* from cover to cover, as well as dozens of other authors along this economic / political spectrum.

Why, you might ask, are you reading about Smith and Marx in a book about the UMC, orphans and vulnerable children? Simply put: economics matter. Economics matters to such a degree that a so-called "Cold War" developed during the later half of the 20th century in which trillions of dollars were spent by both the US and USSR on weapons of mass destruction in a policy widely known as Mutually Assured Destruction (MAD). Economics matters in that issues such as Gross Domestic Product (GDP) and Gross Domestic Product Per Capita (GDPPC) are used to gauge the wealth and health of nations. Economics matters in determining public policies, tax issues, defense spending, governmental programs, foreign aid, health and education. Economics matters.

I would hesitate to encourage any person to read either Smith or Marx's tomes, considering that task more as penance than productive. However, Smith and Marx's economic systems are those that continue to dominate global economies. Familiarity with their writings, along with other leading authors on economic development, will help guide our denomination as we move out into more uncharted territory for most of us.

ADAM SMITH

Adam Smith is considered the father of economics and father of capitalism and his book, *An Inquiry into the Nature and Causes of the Wealth of Nations,* is considered the first real economic book. In this seminal work, first published in 1776, Smith sought to describe why different nations experienced different degrees of wealth: England, in particular, and Europe, in general, were wealthier in the day of Adam Smith than other nations or regions of the world. Smith had reports from the Americas, Africa and Asia, and was able to glean data from these nations for his work. For instance, Smith compared the report of Marco Polo's visits to China towards the end of the 13th century to contemporary reports of his day that seemed to indicate a lack of economic progress and growth in China over the course of approximately 500 years. (Smith 1991:63) Smith wanted to determine what it was that gave each nation its economic advantages or, conversely, held it back.

Smith wrote at the dawn of the Industrial Revolution, generally assigned to the years 1760 – 1830. Although he could neither foresee nor predict the explosive growth and prosperity the Industrial Revolution would bring to Great Britain and other regions of the world, he was able to outline certain themes that are still in use today as tools to describe conditions for or contrary to economic growth. These factors included institutions, incentives, geography and culture.

Adam Smith's work is considered a classic. In the Introduction to a 1991 edition of Smith's work editor D. D. Raphael writes:

> *The Wealth of Nations* is the first of the great classics of economic theory. One can go further and say that, historically speaking, it is the greatest classical work of the social sciences. I do not mean that it revealed fundamental discoveries of enduring truth, like Newton's *Principia* in the physical sciences and Darwin's *Origin of Species* in the biological. The social sciences do not seem to admit that kind of achievement. But *The Wealth of Nations* does resemble those other two books in providing the best model of success in its general field, a work that can inspire every generation by the breadth of its grasp. (Raphael 1991:xiii)

First and foremost, Smith described an economic viewpoint that he thought accounted for England's success based on free markets, *laisse-faire* (from the French – literally, "let do," in economics more like "let alone," "let pass"), natural advantage and limited regulations all governed by an "invisible hand." (Smith 1991:39). He understood national economies as an extension of familiar markets, where buyers and sellers compete for advantage and the furtherance of their respective interests. Smith's evaluation led him to a philosophy of self-interest as an economic engine, as described:

> It is not from the benevolence of the butcher, the brewer, or the baker that we expect our dinner, but from their regard to their own interest. We address ourselves, not to their humanity but to their self-love, and never talk to them of our own necessities but of their advantages. Nobody but a beg-

gar chooses to depend chiefly upon the benevolence of his fellow-citizens. (Smith 1991:13)

Smith described the geographical advantages England enjoyed. He wrote:

> England, on account of the natural fertility of the soil, of the great extent of the sea – coast in proportion to that of the whole country, and of the many navigable rivers which run through it and afford the conveniency of water carriage to some of the most inland parts of it, is perhaps as well fitted by nature as any large country in Europe to be the seat of foreign commerce, of manufacturing for distant sale, and of all the improvements which these can occasion. (Smith 1991:271)

Smith also addressed the issue of the opportunity cost of the military and foreign wars. With a simplicity and directness that speak to contemporary issues as clearly as to his day, Smith writes:

> Such are the people who compose a numerous and splendid court, a great ecclesiastical establishment, great fleets and armies, who in time produce nothing, and in time of war acquire nothing which can compensate the expense of maintaining them, even while the war lasts. Such people, as they themselves produce nothing, are all maintained by the produce of other men's labour . . . . No foreign war of great expense or duration could conveniently be carried on by the exportation of the rude produce of the soil. The expense of sending such a quantity of it to a foreign country as might purchase the pay and provisions of an army would be too great. Few countries produce much more rude produce than what is sufficient for the subsistence of their own inhabitants. To send abroad any great quantity of it, therefore, would be to send abroad a part of the necessary subsistence of the people. (Smith 1991:389)

Along with accolades, the *Wealth of Nations* has also received much criticism. Smith's concept of the "invisible hand," has occasioned much discussion and debate. Joseph Stiglitz, a Nobel Prize winning economist, writes: "the reason that the invisible hand often seems invisible is that it is often not there." (Stiglitz 2006) Stiglitz continues:

> Whenever there are "externalities"—where the actions of an individual have impacts on others for which they do not pay or for which they are not compensated—markets will not work well. Some of the important instances have been long understood—environmental externalities. Markets, by themselves, will produce too much pollution. Markets, by themselves, will also produce too little basic research . . . But recent research has shown that these externalities are pervasive, whenever there is imperfect information or imperfect risk markets—that is always. Government plays an important role in banking and securities regulation, and a host of other areas: some regulation is required to make markets work. Government is needed, almost all would agree, at a minimum to enforce contracts and property rights. (Stiglitz 2006)

Gregory Clark's critique of Smith's philosophy is that the *Wealth of Nations* produces simplistic explanation for complex, dynamic issues. Given the tools Adam Smith was employing in the middle of the 18th Century it is remarkable how prescient and perceptive he was. However, Clark writes:

> The central vision of modern economics, the key message of Adam Smith in 1776 and of his followers, is that people are the same everywhere in their material preferences and aspirations. They behave differently only because of differences in incentives. Given the right circumstances – low tax rates on earnings, security of property and of the person, free markets in goods and labor – growth is guaranteed. The

long Malthusian night persisted because of the inability of
all societies before 1800 to create such institutions. (Clark
2007:145)

The capitalism Smith described is indeed capable of generating great capital, wealth and human progress. A weakness, however, is the inequality
of the distribution of the wealth. We must recognize that the free market
and *laissez faire*, unfettered capitalism have limitations—and that the rules
to govern the market must be established outside and independent of the
market. The reality is that capitalism creates conditions where the very rich
have far more than they need while others struggle. In 2011 the richest 400
Americans had more wealth than half of all US citizens combined (a total
of 150 million persons) During the same year, the top 1% of Americans
owned 42.7 percent of the total wealth of this nation, with the next 19
percent owning 50.3 percent of the wealth leaving the bottom 80 percent
owning only 7 percent of the US wealth.

One of my economic professors put it this way: unfettered, unregu-
lated capitalism is like the game of Monopoly on a grand scale: eventually
all of the money will end up in one person's possession while the others go
bankrupt and are forced to quit. While capitalism provides the incentives
for the generation of wealth, it also contributes to economic inequality at
the local, national, regional and international level. Regulation by forces
outside of the market is necessary to curb the excesses of capitalism and
ensure a more just distribution of the resources within a community.

KARL MARX

Although capitalism enjoys a general level of acceptance among the majority of economists in the United States and throughout the developed world,
an alternative economic system is still in place in many nations around the
world. Known as communism, or Marxism, it was developed, of course,
by Karl Marx. Marx was born approximately 100 years after Adam Smith
(1818 and 1720, respectively) and wrote as the industrial revolution was

revealing its injustices as well as its benefits. "Marx did not discover that capitalism is exploitative. It does not require great intellect to see that the capitalists live off other people's labour." (Arthur 1992:xvii) But Marx took this discovery to an entirely new level, proposing as a more humane alternative a centrally controlled political and economic structure that came to be known synonymously as Communism and/or Marxism.

We need not be afraid of Karl Marx nor his political and economic writing, as were citizens of the US were throughout the Cold War. Marx, like all of us, was a product of the prevailing worldview of his time and culture in which he lived. Karl Marx was an avowed atheist: he believed that capitalism had to be overthrown by violence, and was convinced that his economic principles could work on a broad scale without the individual incentives capitalism was built on. These failings aside, he strove to create a system where human needs were met. Like Adam Smith, Karl Marx was too optimistic that his system would improve the human condition: one can find a great analysis of the characteristics Karl Marx and Adam Smith held in common in Reinhold Niebuhr's book, *The Children of Light and the Children of Darkness*. (Niebuhr 1944)

Marx, working with his associate and colleague Friedrich Engels, published *The Communist Manifesto* in 1848 and *Capital* (*Das Kapital*) in 1867. Although the status and acceptance of *Capital* has risen and fallen since its first publication, its place in history can never be denied. Engels wrote: "'Das Kapital' is often called, on the Continent, 'the Bible of the working class.'" (Engels 1886:30) It is still read by intellectuals across the globe who want to understand the theoretical framework of Marxism and communism. But Marx did less to define his ideal society than to describe the faults of capitalism. Readers of Marx will see a skilled observer and writer of society who described well the horrors of industrial England mid 19th Century. A contemporary of Marx, Charles Dickens, conveyed the human suffering of the industrial revolution in novels, while Marx did this through statistics and economic data.

Where Smith was interested primarily in describing the conditions that fostered development and economic success, Marx's goal was to document the failure of the capitalistic system for the majority of the population and make the case for an alternative economic and political system, namely, communism. Marx claimed that labor, rather than capital, should be the economic foundation of a society and that the means of production should be owned by the state. That Karl Marx was a brilliant scholar and academic intellect of great ability is undeniable: likewise, his analysis of the conditions of his day and the descriptions of the exploitation workers experiences is indisputable.

As the 20th century gave way to the 21st century, however, the political and economic tide turned against Marx. 20th century economist Ludwig Von Mises famously predicted the demise of communism as early as 1951, (Von Mises 1951) and Francis Fukuyama's book *The End of History and the Last Man* (1990) anticipated and celebrated the fall of communism around the world. But communism and centrally controlled economies, the operating system of many nations around the world, including the superpowers of the Soviet Union and China during the 20th Century, have not disappeared completely. If we are to work in the development field we must have an understanding of Karl Marx and the economic worldview he championed, from communism to various forms of socialism.

GREGORY CLARK

Economist Gregory Clark writes: "The basic outline of world economic history is surprisingly simple. Indeed it can be summarized in one diagram: figure 1.1."(Clark 2007:1) Extracted from his book, *A Farewell to Alms*, this diagram traces human progress and development from 1000 BCE to the year 2000 CE and illustrates several broad brush trends:

- Prior to 1800, per-person income remained relatively flat across the planet

- Beginning about the year 1800 CE, spurred by the Industrial Revolution, a number of nations and regions experienced unprecedented economic growth and development.

- Simultaneously, other nations remained mired within the Malthusian Trap, and have even experienced a degree of economic decline. The Malthusian Trap, named after Thomas Malthus, postulates that income will remain stagnant as technology improves because technological advances lead to increased populations that are bound to expand and collapse at regular intervals.

- These separate trajectories have been termed The Great Divergence, coined by Kenneth Pomeranz in his book *The Great Divergence: China, Europe, and the Making of the Modern World Economy*.(Pomeranz 2000)

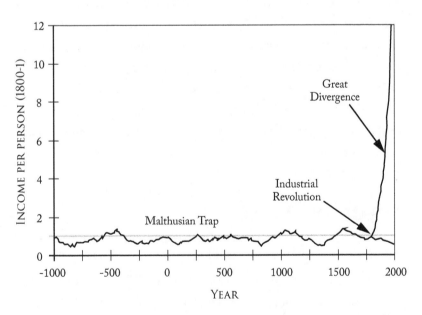

This diagram charts human economic development from approximately 3,000 years ago to the present and shows how the world's people all struggled to escape poverty until approximately the year 1800. Around 1800, the Industrial Revolution led to the "Great Divergence," the attainment of economic wealth and prosperity by some of the world's nations, and a decline in the same categories by other nations. This diagram raises two deceptively simple questions:

1) Why did this happen? (Goldstone 2008)

2) What will it take for the nations who, to date, remain locked in the grip of poverty, to escape this trap and join the other nations on paths of economic growth and prosperity? (Collier 2007)

As in other social sciences, there is a lack of consensus on the answers to these questions within the international development literature. The researcher plunges into a complex, dynamic, fragile and non-linear sea of data that must take into account internal and external factors, geography, political and social institutions, culture, population growth, government, savings, investments and demographics. Gregory Clark and William Easterly, respectively, speak for a variety of economists:

In economics . . . we see . . . that our ability to describe and predict the economic world reached a peak about 1800. In the years since the Industrial Revolution there has been a progressive and continuing disengagement of economic models from any ability to predict differences of income and wealth across time and across countries and regions. (Clark 2007:371)We economists have tried to find the precious object, the key that would enable the poor tropics to become rich. We thought we had found the elixir many different times. The precious objects we offered ranged from foreign aid to investment in machines, from fostering education to controlling population growth, from giving loans conditional on reforms to giving debt relief conditional on reforms. None has delivered as promised. (Easterly 2002:xi)

The pertinent question for this book is: why have some nations been able to generate wealth and prosperity while other nations have not. This question stands behind the orphan and vulnerable children crisis. If all of the nations of the world were as wealthy and developed as the United States, for instance, there would be no orphan crisis today.

JEFFREY SACHS AND WILLIAM EASTERLY

Jeffrey Sachs and William Easterly are contemporary economic rivals based in New York City with differing perspectives on how to reduce global poverty through development. Sachs, a former economic professor at Harvard who traveled the world advising governments on economic matters, now serves as the director of the Earth Institute at Columbia University. Easterly, an employee of the World Bank for twenty years, is now an economic professor at New York University. Together, they are the most visible economists working to describe and eliminate extreme poverty in the developing world. But they sharply disagree on how growth and progress can best be achieved and represent conflicting economic theories.

Easterly describes these global conditions:

Almost three billion people live on less than two dollars a day, adjusted for purchasing power. Eight hundred and forty million people in the world don't have enough to eat. Ten million children die every year from easily preventable diseases. AIDS is killing three million people a year and is still spreading. One billion people in the world lack access to clean water; two billion lack access to sanitation. One billion adults are illiterate. About a quarter of the children in poor countries do not finish primary school. (Easterly 2006:8)

Easterly reminds his readers of one reality: in the past 60 years, $2.3 trillion has been given to international development organizations and governments to assist Africa, and yet the conditions listed above continue. The aid-financed investment fetish has led us astray on our quest for growth for fifty years. The model should finally be laid to rest . . . giving aid on the basis of the financing gap creates perverse incentives for the recipient, as was recognized long ago. The financing gap is larger, and aid larger, the lower the saving of the recipient. This creates incentives against the recipient's marshaling its own resources for development. (Easterly 2002:44)

Aid-financed investment has failed, according to Easterly, because it fails the most elementary theories of economics:

What is the basic principle of economics? As a wise elder once told me. 'People do what they get paid to do: what they don't get paid to do, they don't do.' A wonderful book by Steven Landsburg, *The Armchair Economist*, distills the principle more concisely: "People respond to incentives; all the rest is commentary.' (Easterly 2002:xii)

Easterly's solution? Stop giving foreign aid to governments and discover ways to help individuals who are striving to improve their lives. "Discard your patronizing confidence that you know how to solve other people's problems better than they do. Don't try to fix governments or societies. Don't invade other countries, or send arms to one of the brutal armies in a civil war . . . Once the West is willing to aid individuals rather than governments, some conundrums that tie foreign aid up in knots are resolved." (Easterly 2006:368)

But even Easterly acknowledges that positive steps have been taken. He writes:

Foreign aid likely contributed to some notable successes on a global scale, such as dramatic improvements in health and education indicators in poor countries. Life expectancy in the typical poor country has risen from forty-eight years to sixty-eight years over the past four decades. Forty years ago, 131 out of every 1,000 babies born in poor countries died before reaching their first birthday. Today, 36 out of every 1,000 babies dies before their first birthday. (Easterly 2006:176)

Jeffrey Sachs, who has also provided private tutoring to rock star and philanthropist Bono, makes the case that the developed Western nations can, with minimal sacrifices, help provide the relief necessary to save millions of lives and create long-term, sustainable economic projects. For instance:

The World Bank estimates that meeting basic needs requires $1.08 per day per person, measured in 1993 purchasing-power adjusted prices. . . According to the Bank's estimates, 1.1 billion people lived below the $1.08 level as of 2001, with an average income of $0.77 per day, or $281 per year. More important, the poor had a shortfall relative to basic needs of $0.31 per day, or $113 per year. Worldwide, the total income shortfall of the poor in 2001 was therefore $113 per year per person multiplied by 1.1 billion people, of $124 billion. (Sachs 2005:290)"plainCitation":"(Sachs 2005:290

Further, "the end of extreme poverty would also require less than one percent of the annual income of the rich world to finance the crucial investments needed in the poorest countries to extricate them from the poverty trap (and even that modest transfer to the poor would be temporary, perhaps lasting only until 2025)." (Sachs 2008:12)

Sachs' solution seems simple. Visitors' to African game reserves want to see the "Big Five:" elephants, lions, buffalo, rhinoceros and leopards. The road towards economic security for Africa lies in Sach's "Big Five for Economic Development:"

1. Agricultural inputs: i.e. fertilizers, irrigation, storage facilities, and improved seeds.
2. Investments in basic health: more village clinics, mosquito nets, and basic vaccinations.
3. Investments in education: Meals at school should be provided, vocational training, computer literacy.
4. Power, transportation and communication services: electricity, village trucks, and mobile phones.
5. Safe drinking water and sanitation: new wells and latrines.

How can this be achieved? According to Sachs, through temporary, aid financed investment.

> These burdens [poverty trap] are surmountable, and at a remarkably low cost. Food production can be increased; disease can be controlled; education and literacy can be expanded to ensure universal coverage of the young; and infrastructure – especially roads, power, water, and sanitation – can be put in place. Indeed, these things can happen rapidly if the projects can be implemented. While in a handful of cases the limiting factor is poor governance, in most cases it is finance. The poor know what to do but are too poor to do it . . . That is where foreign assistance comes in. A temporary boost of aid over the course of several years, if properly invested, can lead to a permanent rise in productivity. That boost, in turn, leads to self-sustaining growth. The logical chain is the following:

Temporary aid → Boost of productivity → Rise of saving and investment → Sustained growth

Sachs and Easterly symbolize the competing division between capitalistic economists who favor top-down, institutional-led projects and programs (Sachs) and bottom up, incentive-based programs and projects for individual (Easterly). Today Sachs advises G-8 leaders to increase their foreign aid budgets to help solve extreme poverty. Easterly remains extremely skeptical of top – down, government led programs and is looking for individuals on the grass roots level who, unimpeded by governments, will help find and build sustainable economic systems.

I am convinced that the answer falls somewhere between Easterly and Sachs with a combination from each. Governmental, top-down programs and activities can be successful and history is filled with examples, from the Egyptian pyramids to the US efforts to place human beings on the moon and return them successfully. But governmental, top down programs have limits. Easterly's answer is to create incentives for growth among government, donors and individuals. This is where the institutional church can be of help. We have thousands of churches in the US that have material resources we can and, if we are true to John Wesley, should use to help our brothers and sisters in need (thus helping ourselves as well). Likewise, there are thousands of churches who could use these resources to provide health and educational opportunities for their people and help break the poverty cycle.

DEVELOPMENT THEORIES

The research presented thus far, however, still does not answer this basic question posed by Samuel Huntington:

> In the early 1990s, I happened to come across economic data on Ghana and South Korea in the early 1960s, and I was astonished to see how similar their economies were then. These two countries had roughly comparable levels of manufacturing, and services; and overwhelmingly primary product exports, with South Korea producing a few manu-

factured goods. Also, they were receiving comparable levels of economic aid. Thirty years later, South Korea had become an industrial giant with the fourteenth largest economy in the world, multinational corporations, major exports of automobiles, electronic equipment, and other sophisticated manufactures, and a per capita income approximating that of Greece. Moreover, it was on its way to the consolidation of democratic institutions. No such changes had occurred in Ghana, whose per capita GNP was now about one-fifteenth that of South Korea's. *How could this extraordinary difference in development be explained?* (Huntington 1996:xv)

An answer has not been given to this question because, in part, no consensus has been reached. The best anyone can suggest is that the differences in development nations experiences is a dynamic, complex combination of economic, technology, political, cultural, geographical and random factors. Never the less, there are several leading theories regarding the process of development which will be explored now.

JARED DIAMOND

In *Guns, Germs and Steel* Jared Diamond sought to answer a question posed to him in 1972 by a friend from New Guinea named Yali, who asked: "Why is it that you white people developed so much cargo [technological and consumer goods] and brought it to New Guinea, but we black people had little cargo of our own?" (Diamond 1999:14) Diamond answers this question a few pages later in a simple, summary sentence of his 500-page book: "History followed different courses for different peoples because of differences among peoples' environments, not because of biological differences among peoples themselves." (Diamond 1999:25) With meticulous research and careful analysis, Diamond makes the case that geography and location fed the Euro – Asian development cycle. The natural resources, native plants, animal species and weather patterns of Euro-Asia led to the development of technological innovation and immunity from certain diseases which spurred the virtual conquest of the rest of the world by this region. In Diamond's opinion, "Europe's colonization of Africa had nothing to do with differences between European and African peoples themselves, as white racists assume. Rather, it was due to accidents of geography and bio-geography . . . that is, the different historical trajectories of Africa and Europe stem ultimately from differences in real estate." (Diamond 1999:401)

Diamond's research suggests that while Europe emerged as the dominant region of the world through these geographical advantages, the technology and resources to replicate these developments can and will work now in other parts of the world. But because Europe developed them first it had a major head start and advantage over others that continues to be exploited to this very day.

MODERNIZATION THEORY

W. W. Rostow's book, *The Stages of Economic Growth: A Non-Communist Manifesto*, was published in 1960 and instantly became a classic. Rostow identified five stages of growth nations experienced, being:

1. **Traditional Societies**: Defined as pre-Newtonian and pre-technology, these societies lack scientific conceptions of the world and do not have a concept of economic growth. "The central fact about the traditional society was that a ceiling existed on the level of attainable output per head."

2. **Preconditions to Take Off**: Rostow sees in this stage a commitment to secular education, the establishment of banks and a stable currency, and a concept of manufacturing. "The preconditions for take-off were initially developed, in a clearly marked way, in Western Europe of the late seventeenth and early eighteenth centuries as the insights of modern science began to be translated into new production functions in both agriculture and industry, in a setting given dynamism by the lateral expansion of

world markets and the international competition for them . . .
The idea spreads not merely that economic progress is possible,
but that economic progress is a necessary condition for some
other purpose, judged to be good."

3. **Take off**. "In Britain and well-endowed parts of the world
populated substantially from Britain (the United States, Canada
etc.) the proximate stimulus for take-off was mainly (but not
wholly) technological." Here, the economy is clearly in transition that Rostow uses to describe the evolution towards a modern economy.

4. **Drive to Maturity**. A mature economy must be diversified.
"Formally, we can define maturity as the stage in which an
economy demonstrates the capacity to move beyond the original
industries which powered its take-off and to absorb and to apply efficiently over a very wide range of its resources – if not the
whole range – the most advanced fruits of modern technology."

5. **Age of High Mass Consumption**. This is the stage of contemporary comfort experienced by many western nations where
consumers concentrate on durable goods: "As societies achieved
maturity in the twentieth century two things happened: real income per head rose to a point where a large number of persons
gained a command over consumption which transcended basic food, shelter, and clothing; and the structure of the working force changed in ways which increased not only the proportion of urban to total population, but also the proportion of the
population working in offices or in skilled factory jobs – aware
of and anxious to acquire the consumption fruits of a mature
economy." (Rostow 1990)

Rostow's model and stages of economic growth has come to be identified
with Modernization Theory. The origins of this theory can be traced to 19th
Century writers Emile Durkheim and Max Weber. Durkheim and Weber,

students of Darwin, bring evolution, natural selection and survival of the fittest in a world of scarce competition into their sociological writings.

Durkheim's major work, *The Division of Labour in Society*, suggests that there are two kinds of societies in the world, these being "traditional" and "modern." Traditional societies are based on an agrarian economy where the majority of people live in villages and there is little difference between one village and another. Modern societies evolve out of traditional societies and differ in the increasing population totals and density. To survive under such conditions, the division of labor and specialization is required. (Durkheim, Halls, and Durkheim 1984)

Max Weber's most important work was *The Protestant Ethic and the Spirit of Capitalism*. Here Weber argued that the rational economic activities of Western societies were part of a cultural process most closely identified with the Protestant Reformer John Calvin. Steady profits and the accumulation of capital is brought about by the dedication to a variety of tasks, including economic efficiency and a continual effort to provide services better than one's competition. "In their different ways Durkheim and Weber have provided many of the basic themes of present day modernisation theory in particular their contrast between traditional and modern societies." (Webster 1990:46)

THEORIES OF UNDERDEVELOPMENT

Modernisation Theory is based on the writings of Durkheim and Weber: Underdevelopment Theory is based on class conflict and returns to the writings of Karl Marx. Countries that have yet to develop are considered, under the modernization theory, to lack the necessary value system and entrepreneurial skills. Underdevelopment theory pays more attention to the inequalities of power and class conflict. Andrew Webster writes:

> The dominant class, the capitalists, own and control the means of production and thereby exploit the subordinate working class . . . This state of affairs cannot be changed

without removing the class structure itself. This clearly means challenging the position of the dominant capitalist class . . . Marx describes how the exploitation of workers' labour is not limited by national boundaries. Capitalist will seek to take possession of labour – power abroad as well. Marx refers to that time from about the sixteenth to the late eighteenth centuries when wealthy merchants built up their fortunes in western Europe by plundering the raw materials and labour of other nations." (Webster 1990:69)

Nathan Nunn asks whether Africa's economic woes in the second half of the twentieth century can be linked to the tragedy of the slave trade and colonialism and answers affirmatively. (Nunn 2008:1) "I find that the importance of the slave trade for contemporary development is a result of its detrimental impact on the formation of domestic institutions, such as the security of private property, the quality of the judicial system, and the overall rule of law. This is the channel through which the slave trade continues to matter today." (Nunn 2008:1) Patrick Manning wrote "Slavery was corruption: it involved theft, bribery, and exercise of brute force as well as ruses. Slavery thus may be seen as one source of precolonial origins for modern corruption." (Manning 1990)

Jeffrey Sachs summarizes African history during the past 500 years like this:

> Three centuries of slave trade, from about 1500 to the early 1800s, were followed by a century of brutal colonial rule. Far from lifting Africa economically, the colonial era left Africa bereft of educated citizens and leaders, basic infrastructure, and public health facilities. The borders of the newly independent states followed the arbitrary lines of the former empires, dividing ethnic groups, ecosystems, watersheds, and resource deposits in arbitrary ways.

As soon as the colonial period ended, Africa became a pawn in the cold war. Western cold warriors, and the operatives in the CIA and counterpart agencies in Europe, opposed African leaders who preached nationalism, sought aid from the Soviet Union, or demanded better terms on Western investments in African minerals and energy deposits. (Sachs 2005:189)"plainCitation":"(Sachs 2005:189

African writer Ahmad Abubakar also points to slavery and colonialism as the issues behind Africa's economic woes and dependence upon development aid. He writes: "The slave trade took its toll of the African labor force, causing loss of production to Africa and a corresponding gain in production for the British, the Portuguese, the Spaniards, the French, and the North American colonialist, just to mention a few. If the structure and mode of production had been left to develop autochthonously, perhaps the story for Africa would have been different today. The fundamental and immediate objective of colonialism was exploitation for reasons that are common knowledge." (Abubakar 1989:124)

Africa's struggle with colonialism was longer and worse than that experienced by the US. The United States, Australia and New Zealand, for example, are considered classic examples of "settler colonialism," whereas colonialism in most of Africa, India and other parts of Asia are examples of "exploitation colonialism." (Elkins and Pedersen 2005) Unlike America under colonialism, Africans were never seen as equals to Europeans. Africans were never allowed access to education, weapons or governmental positions. (Shillington 1995) Technical superiority allowed the European nations to conquer and control. Vincent Khapoya writes about the colonial powers attention to the economics of African colonization. Systematically, Europeans were intent on land acquisition, enforced labor, introduction of cash crops even when the local populations were in need of food and the continuation of Africa as a source of raw material for Europe. Africa, through the concerted public polices of

Europe, was denied the opportunity to develop. (Khapoya 1994:134–150) "Europe," according to Frantz Fanon, "is literally the creation of the Third World." (Fanon 1968:102) Fanon's argument reasons that Europe was built on the back of Africa and other Third World nations who themselves were plundered, robbed and pillaged.

Fantu Chero writes:

> More than any other region in the world, Africa has paid a high price for the globalizing policies of rival capitalistic powers as they have striven to expand the geographical bounds of capital. Starting with the slave trade in 1650, and continuing under colonial rule after the Berlin Conference of 1884, the continent was heavily drawn into the centres of capitalistic accumulation, but always as a subordinate partner whose primary role was to contribute to the development of the metropolitan powers. (Cheru 2002:2)

Following African independence, remnants of the colonial system remained in place. Karuti Kanyinga, Odenda Lumumba and Kojo Sebastian Amanor write regarding the residue of Kenya's colonial experience:

> At independence in 1963, Kenya inherited a highly skewed system of landownership that could not contribute to poverty reduction and sustainable development. Despite land being central to the decolonization struggle, post-independence Kenya has retained, virtually unaltered, the colonial legal framework and ordinance for land administration, for the protection of private land rights and the regulation of access to land. This has served to . . . entrench private ownership of land and in the process has ratified the titles of colonial settlers as absolute owners of expropriated land. This has sealed the fate of the landless and squatters, thereby intensifying the tenure insecurity of the poor. (Karuti, Lumumba, and Amanor 2008:100)

Africa was not the only region to be exploited by the Western powers through slavery and colonialization, which also took place in Asia, Central and South America, but it is the quintessential example used by advocates of the underdevelopment theory. Slavery and colonialization, this theory argues, has now been replaced by neo-colonialism whereby multi-national corporations (MNCs) "establish subsidiaries outside the US in many nations, particularly in those offering cheap labour." Webster writes:

> According to this view, therefore, the growth of the MNCs is the principal feature of neo-colonialism, as corporations increase their economic grip on the raw materials and labour power of Third World, nominally independent, countries. MNCs use their world-wide business structure to control production from the raw material, through the processing, to the final retail sales. The MNC represents, therefore, the increasing concentration of capital and the integration of production on a world scale. (Webster 1990:80)

Building off the Underdevelopment Theory Model is the Dependency Theory. Dependency Theory is based on the idea that the ongoing poverty experienced in the developing nations is more truly described by their "dependency" on the developed nations.

> Dependency theory originated in the 1960s through the work of a number of academics and development economists who were particularly concerned over the continuing economic failure of Latin American countries. They dismissed the notions of modernization theory that a lack of development could be attributed to a deficiency in appropriate modernizing values and that exposure to advanced industrial countries could only be of positive benefit to the Third World. Instead they argued that the massive and persistent poverty in countries like Argentina, Peru, Chile and

Brazil was caused by exposure to the economic and political influences of the advanced countries. (Webster 1990:84–85)

DO NO HARM

In 1999 Mary Anderson published *Do No Harm: How Aid Can Support Peace – Or War*. This book is an attempt to merge the Latin phrase *primum non nocere* ("first, do no harm" – used in the Hippocratic Oath) with international development. The book claims that foreign aid, even when conducted under the best altruistic motives, under the wrong circumstances can create harmful effects. This accessible, multifaceted book presents development and foreign aid organizations with a challenging question: are your efforts building peace or building war? The book is based on five case studies of development programs in regions of potential or actual conflict: Tajikistan, Lebanon, Burundi, India and Somalia. Anderson writes: "When international assistance is given in the context of a violent conflict, it becomes a part of that context and thus also of the conflict."(Anderson 1999:1) She continues:

> We believe international aid is a good thing. We think the world is a better place because when some people suffer, other people who are able to take actions to help lessen that suffering do so. The challenge we see for aid workers – and for the large number of generous and caring individuals who support their work with financial and material contributions – is to figure out how to do the good they mean to do without inadvertently undermining local strengths, promoting dependency, and allowing aid resources to be misused in the pursuit of war. (Anderson 1999:2)

Anderson's research and data were collected during the 1990's: her research is primarily concerned with Government Organizations (GOs – such as USAID) and Non-Government Organizations (NGOs – such as World Vision or Mennonite Central Committee). She reminds her readers that:

> The majority of today's wars are fought within national
> boundaries rather than between nations or states. They
> are fought between groups that have a history of living to-
> gether and share a language, religion, and culture. They are
> fought by people who have worked together, been educated
> together, and sometimes intermarried. People at war today
> are fighting former friends, neighbors, coworkers, co-wor-
> shippers, and sometimes even family members. (Anderson
> 1999:11)

Therefore, contemporary conflicts are usually complex, multi-layered civil
wars that "are also characterized by local capacities for peace and by connectors that interlink the people who fight." (Anderson 1999:23) Anderson identifies individuals and institutions she labels "Local Capacities for
Peace Project (LCPP)" as those who are connectors who will increase the
connection and capacity for peace. Likewise, there are individuals and institutions that have the capacities for war and are sources of tension that
become dividers. A critical analytic framework must be established that:

1. Identifies the dividers, tensions, and war capacities in the con-
    text of conflict and assess their importance.
2. Identifies the connectors and capacities for peace within the
    same context.
3. Identifies the characteristics of the aid agency and its program
    and the impact on the dividers, tensions and war capacities as
    well as the connectors and capacity for peace.

Demographic Transition Model

Finally, I want to include a short section on what is known as the theoretical Demographic Transition Model, or DTM. Warren Thompson
coined this terminology in 1929 after studying birth and death rates in
developed countries over a period of 200 years. DMT provides a formal

description of four phases of demographic transition through a series of related transitions that occur over time. The focus of the DMT is on the total effect of the two most important factors: mortality (death rate) and fertility (birth rate).

☐ Phase I is known as the Preindustrial: in this stage both mortality and fertility are high. There are many births, but the high death rate limits the population growth.

☐ Phase II is the Transitional Phase: in this stage the death rate begins to decline as technological advantages are introduced. People begin to live longer, but the birth rate remains high leading to an increase in population growth.

☐ Phase III is the Industrial Phase, where the death rate and birth rate both tend to decrease. The population will continue to grow as there will be a period when new births, even at a decreased number, out pace mortality as the population lives longer.

☐ Phase IV is the Post-Industrial Phase: in this final phase the death rate is low and the birth rate continues to decline. In theory, the birth and death rates match each other so that there is population stabilization through zero population growth: data collected from some post-industrial societies indicates a continuing decline in birth rates leading to a negative population growth rate and declining population base.

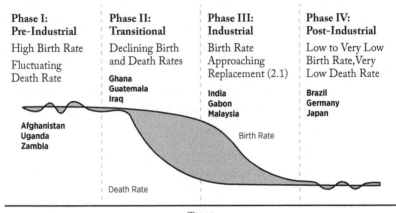

Phase I: Pre-Industrial	Phase II: Transitional	Phase III: Industrial	Phase IV: Post-Industrial
High Birth Rate Fluctuating Death Rate	Declining Birth and Death Rates **Ghana** **Guatemala** **Iraq**	Birth Rate Approaching Replacement (2.1) **India** **Gabon** **Malaysia**	Low to Very Low Birth Rate,Very Low Death Rate **Brazil** **Germany** **Japan**

TIME

This chart depicts the population characteristics within the four phases. I include information about the Demographic Transition Model with this hope: as we care for orphans and vulnerable children there will initially be an increase in global population as less children die around the planet. Properly cared for, educated and equipped, these children can become tomorrow's leaders capable of breaking the poverty trap and leading their nations into phases of zero population growth, something essential as we deal with an ever growing stress on the world's resources.

CONCLUSION

Although economists and development scholars may not agree on how and why this spectacular chasm has been created between the rich and poor nations, they do agree that this enormous gap exists. Dani Rodrik writes: "Average income in Sierra Leone, which is the poorest country in the world for which we have data, is almost one hundred times lower than that in Luxembourg, the world's richest country. Nearly two-thirds of the world's population lives in countries where average income is only one-tenth the U.S. level." (Rodrik 2003:1) Although no satisfactory answer has yet been given to the basic question, "How do we make sense of this disparity," it is not from a lack of trying. Assuming that this disparity and the existence of extreme poverty in many parts of the world is a concern to the people of faith in the developed nations, further research and models need to be developed so that a more equitable distribution of the world's resources can be achieved.

This literature review, or extended, annotated bibliography of international developmental, is included simply as the means in which to introduce readers to the primary themes running through this ongoing discussion. As already mentioned, I would not encourage any readers of this book to pick up copies of *The Wealth of Nations* or *Capital* and begin reading. But I would encourage readers to become familiar with at least the writings of William Easterly (*The Elusive Quest for Growth* and *The White Man's Burden*), Jeffrey Sachs (*The End of Poverty* and *Common Wealth*), Mary Anderson (*Do No Harm*) and Paul Collier (*The Bottom Billion*).

REFERENCES

Abubakar, Ahmad. 1989. Africa and the Challenge of Development: Acquiescence and Dependency versus Freedom and Development. New York: Praeger.

Agyo, Al-hassan Abdullahi. 2014. "Nigeria Partnership Orphanage Announces Secondary School Graduation of First Class of Students." Great Plains UMC Website.

Alexander, Neil, ed. 2012. The Book of Discipline of the United Methodist Church. Nashville, Tenn: United Methodist Publishing House.

Anderson, Mary B. 1999. Do No Harm: How Aid Can Support Peace–or War. Boulder, Colo.: Lynne Rienner Publishers.

Arthur, C. J. 1992. "Introduction." in Mars's Capital, edited by C. J. Arthur. London: Lawrence & Wishart.

Calaprice, Alice. 2005. The New Quotable Einstein. Princeton, N.J: Princeton University Press.

Carder, Ken and Council of UMC Bishops. 1996. Children and Poverty: An Episcopal Initiative. Biblical and Theological Foundations. Nashville, Tenn: The United Methodist Publishing House. Retrieved (http://www.ministrywith.org/files/91/ChildrenPovertyEpiscopalInitiative.pd).

Cheru, Fantu. 2002. African Renaissance: Roadmaps to the Challenge of Globalization. London; New York; Cape Town; New York: Zed Books; D. Philip; Distributed in the USA exclusively by Palgrave.

Clark, Gregory. 2007. A Farewell to Alms: A Brief Economic History of the World. Princeton: Princeton University Press.

Collier, Paul. 2007. The Bottom Billion: Why the Poorest Countries Are Failing and What Can Be Done about It. Oxford; New York: Oxford University Press.

Collins, James C. 2001. Good to Great: Why Some Companies Make the Leap--and Others Don't. 1st ed. New York, NY: HarperBusiness.

Diamond, Jared M. 1999. Guns, Germs, and Steel: The Fates of Human Societies. 1st Norton pbk. New York: W.W. Norton & Co.

Durkheim, Emile, W. D. Halls, and Emile Durkheim. 1984. The Division of Labour in Society. Houndmills, Basingstoke, Hampshire: Macmillan.

Easterly, William Russell. 2002. The Elusive Quest for Growth: Economists' Adventures and Misadventures in the Tropics. Cambridge, Mass.: MIT Press.

Easterly, William Russell. 2006. The White Man's Burden: Why the West's Efforts to Aid the Rest Have Done so Much Ill and so Little Good. New York: Penguin Press.

Elkins, Caroline and Susan Pedersen. 2005. Settler Colonialism in the Twentieth Century: Projects, Practices, Legacies. New York: Routledge.

Engels, Fredrich. 1886. "Editor's Preface to the First English Translation." in Capital. New York: Random House, Inc.

Fanon, Frantz. 1968. The Wretched of the Earth. New York: Grove Press.

Finke, Roger and Rodney Stark. 1992. The Churching of America, 1776-1990: Winners and Losers in Our Religious Economy. New Brunswick, N.J: Rutgers University Press.

Goldstone, Jack. 2008. Why Europe? The Rise of the West in World History, 1500 - 1850. New York: McGraw Hill Higher Education.

Heitzenrater, Richard. 2002. "The Poor and the People Called Methodists." in The Poor and the People Called Methodists, edited by R. Heitzenrater. Nashville, Tenn: Kingswood Books.

Heitzenrater, Richard P. 2013. Wesley and the People Called Methodists. Nashville: Abingdon Press.

Hillery, Maggie. 2011. "Home Nourishes Body, Soul of Nigerian Youth." UMC Communications. Retrieved (http://www.umc.org/news-and-media/home-nourishes-body-soul-of-nigerian-young).

Huntington, Samuel P. 1996. The Clash of Civilizations and the Remaking of World Order. 1st Touchstone. New York: Simon & Schuster.

Jennings, Theodore W. 1990. Good News to the Poor: John Wesley's Evangelical Economics. Nashville: Abingdon Press.

Karuti, Kanyinga, Odenda Lumumba, and Kojo Sebastian Amanor. 2008. "The Struggle for Sustainable Land Management and Democratic Development in Kenya: A History of Greed and Grievances." in Land & Sustainable Development in Africa, edited by K. S. Amanor and S. Moyo. London and New York: Zed Books.

Khapoya, Vincent B. 1994. The African Experience: An Introduction. Englewood Cliffs, N.J.: Prentice Hall.

Kruse, Kevin. 2015. "How Business Made Us Christian." New York Times, March 15.

Lankford, John. 1963. "Methodism 'Over the Top': The Joint Centenary Movement, 1917-1925." Methodist History 10(October):27–37.

Luccock, Halford Edward. 1949. The Story of Methodism. New York: Abingdon-Cokesbury Press.

Maddox, Randy. 2002. "Visit the Poor: John Wesley, the Poor, and the Sanctification of Believers." in The Poor and the People Called Methodists, edited by R. Heitzenrater. Nashville, Tenn: Kingswood Books.

Manning, Patrick. 1990. Slavery and African Life: Occidental, Oriental, and African Slave Trades. Cambridge; New York: Cambridge University Press.

Niebuhr, H. Richard. 1956. Christ and Culture. 1st Harper torch-book ed. New York: Harper & Brothers.

Niebuhr, Reinhold. 1944. The Children of Light and the Children of Darkness. New York,: C. Scribner's sons.

Norwood, Frederick Abbott. 1974. The Story of American Methodism; a History of the United Methodists and Their Relations. Nashville: Abingdon Press.

Nuechterlein, James. 1988. "Athens and Jerusalem in Indiana." The American Scholar 57(3):353–68.

Nunn, Nathan. 2008. "The Long - Term Effects of Africa's Slave Trades." Quarterly Journal of Economics 123(1):139–76.

Oursler, Kay. 2011. "Mother of African Orphans: Kay Oursler." United Methodist Communication. Retrieved (http://www.umc.org/news-and-media/mother-for-african-orphans-kay-oursler).

Phillips, Kevin P. 2006. American Theocracy: The Peril and Politics of Radical Religion, Oil, and Borrowed Money in the 21st Century. New York: Viking.

Pomeranz, Kenneth. 2000. The Great Divergence: Europe, China, and the Making of the Modern World Economy. Princeton, N.J.: Princeton University Press.

Raphael, D. D. 1991. "Introduction." in The Wealth of Nations. New York: Alfred Knopf.

Rieger, Joerg. 2002. "Between God and the Poor: Rethinking the Means of Grace in the Wesleyan Tradition." in The Poor and the People Called Methodists 1729 - 1999. Nashville, Tenn: Kingswood Books.

Rodrik, Dani. 2003. In Search of Prosperity: Analytic Narratives on Economic Growth. Princeton, N.J. ; Oxford: Princeton University Press.

Rostow, W. W. 1990. The Stages of Economic Growth: A Non-Communist Manifesto. 3rd ed. Cambridge England; New York: Cambridge University Press.

Sachs, Jeffrey. 2005. The End of Poverty: Economic Possibilities for Our Time. New York: Penguin Press.

Sachs, Jeffrey. 2008. Common Wealth: Economics for a Crowded Planet. New York: Penguin Press.

Shaller, Lyle. 2004. The Ice Cube Is Melting. Nashville, Tenn: Abingdon Press.

Shillington, Kevin. 1995. History of Africa. Rev. New York: St. Martin's Press.

Smith, Adam. 1991. The Wealth of Nations. New York: Knopf: Distributed by Random House.

Stiglitz, Joseph E. 2006. Making Globalization Work. 1st ed. New York: W.W. Norton & Co.

Subbarao, Kalanidhi and Diane Coury. 2004. Reaching Out to Arfica's Orphans: A Framework for Public Action. Washington, D.C: The World Bank.

Trickle Up Staff. 2014. "Living on Less Than $1.25 a Day." Understanding Poverty. Retrieved November 9, 2014 (http://www.trickleup.org/poverty/extreme-poverty.cfm).

UNICEF Staff. 2013. "UNICEF Annual Report 2013 | UNICEF Publications." UNICEF. Retrieved October 13, 2014 (http://www.unicef.org/publications/index_73682.html).

United Nations. 1995. World Summit for Social Development. Copenhagen, Denmark: United Nations. Retrieved November 9, 2014 (http://www.un.org/documents/ga/conf166/aconf166-9.htm).

Von Mises, Ludwig. 1951. Socialism: An Economic and Sociological Analysis. New. New Haven,: Yale University Press.

Warner, Laceye. 2008. "Spreading Scriptural Holiness: Theology and Practices of Early Methodist for the Contemporary Church." The Asbury Journal 63(1):115–38. Retrieved November 29, 2014 (http://place.asburyseminary.edu/asburyjournal/vol63/iss1/7/).

Webster, Andrew. 1990. Introduction to the Sociology of Development. 2nd ed. Atlantic Highlands, NJ: Humanities Press International.

Weinberg, Steven. 1999. "A Designer Universe." in Conference on Cosmic Design. Washington, D.C.

Wesley, John. 1777. "The Letters of John Wesley." Wesley Center On Line. Retrieved (http://wesley.nnu.edu/john-wesley/the-letters-of-john-wesley/wesleys-letters-1790b/).

Wesley, John. 1790. "The Letters of John Wesley." Wesley Center On Line. Retrieved (http://wesley.nnu.edu/john-wesley/the-letters-of-john-wesley/wesleys-letters-1790b/).

Wesley, John. 1830. The Works of John Wesley, A. M. 3rd ed. edited by J. Mason. London: John Mason.

Wesley, John. 1831. The Works of the Reverend John Wesley, A.M. edited by J. Emory. New York: J. Collard.

Wesley, John. 1850. The Works of the Reverend John Wesley. edited by Emory. New York: Lane & Scott.

Wesley, John. 1984a. "On Zeal." in The Works of John Wesley, vol. 3. Nashville: Abingdon Press.

Wesley, John. 1984b. "Sermon on the Mount, Discourse VII." in The Works of John Wesley, vol. 1. Nashville: Abingdon Press.

Wesley, John. 1985a. "Catholic Spirit." in The Works of John Wesley, vol. 2. Nashville: Abingdon Press.

Wesley, John. 1985b. "On the Death of the Rev. Mr. George Whitefield." in The Works of John Wesley, vol. 2. Nashville: Abingdon Press.

Wesley, John. 1985c. "The Mystery of Iniquity." in The Works of John Wesley, vol. 2. Nashville: Abingdon Press.

Wesley, John. 1986a. "On Dress." in The Works of John Wesley, vol. 3. Nashville: Abingdon Press.

Wesley, John. 1986b. "The Dangers of Riches." in The Works of John Wesley. Nashville: Abingdon Press.

Wesley, John. 1987a. "A Farther Appeal to Men of Reason and Religion." in The Works of John Wesley, vol. 11. Nashville: Abingdon Press.

Wesley, John. 1987b. "An Earnest Appeal to Men of Reason and Religion." in The Works of John Wesley, vol. 11. Nashville: Abingdon Press.

Wesley, John. 1987c. "Causes of the Inefficacy of Christians." in The Works of John Wesley, vol. 4. Nashville: Abingdon Press.

Wesley, John. 1987d. "Letters." in The Works of John Wesley, vol. 25. Nashville: Abingdon Press.

Wesley, John. 1987e. "On the Dangers of Increasing Wealth." in The Works of John Wesley, vol. 4. Nashville: Abingdon Press.

Wesley, John. 1989a. "A Plain Account of the People Called Methodist." in The Works of John Wesley, vol. 9. Nashville: Abingdon Press.

Wesley, John. 1989b. "Thoughts Upon Methodism." in The Works of John Wesley, vol. 9. Nashville: Abingdon Press.

Wesley, John. 1990. "Journals and Diaries." in The Works of John Wesley, vol. 19. Nashville: Abingdon Press.

Wesley, John. 1991a. "Journals and Diaries." in The Works of John Wesley, vol. 20. Nashville: Abingdon Press.

Wesley, John. 1991b. "Journals and Diaries." in The Works of John Wesley, vol. 20. Nashville: Abingdon Press.

Wesley, John. 1992. Journals and Diaries. Nashville: Abingdon Press.

Wesley, John. 1995. "Journals and Diaries." in The Works of John Wesley, vol. 23. Nashville: Abingdon Press.

Whetten, Kathryn et al. 2009. "A Comparison of the Wellbeing of Orphans and Abandoned Children Ages 6–12 in Institutional and Community-Based Care Settings in 5 Less Wealthy Nations." PLoS ONE 4(12):e8169. Retrieved March 21, 2015 (http://dx.doi.org/10.1371/journal.pone.0008169).

Wilke, Richard B. 1986. And Are We yet Alive?: The Future of the United Methodist Church. Nashville: Abingdon Press.

W. Watt. 1974. Muhammad : Prophet and Statesman. London: New York.

Printed in the USA
CPSIA information can be obtained
at www.ICGtesting.com
JSHW022327140824
68134JS00019B/1345

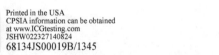